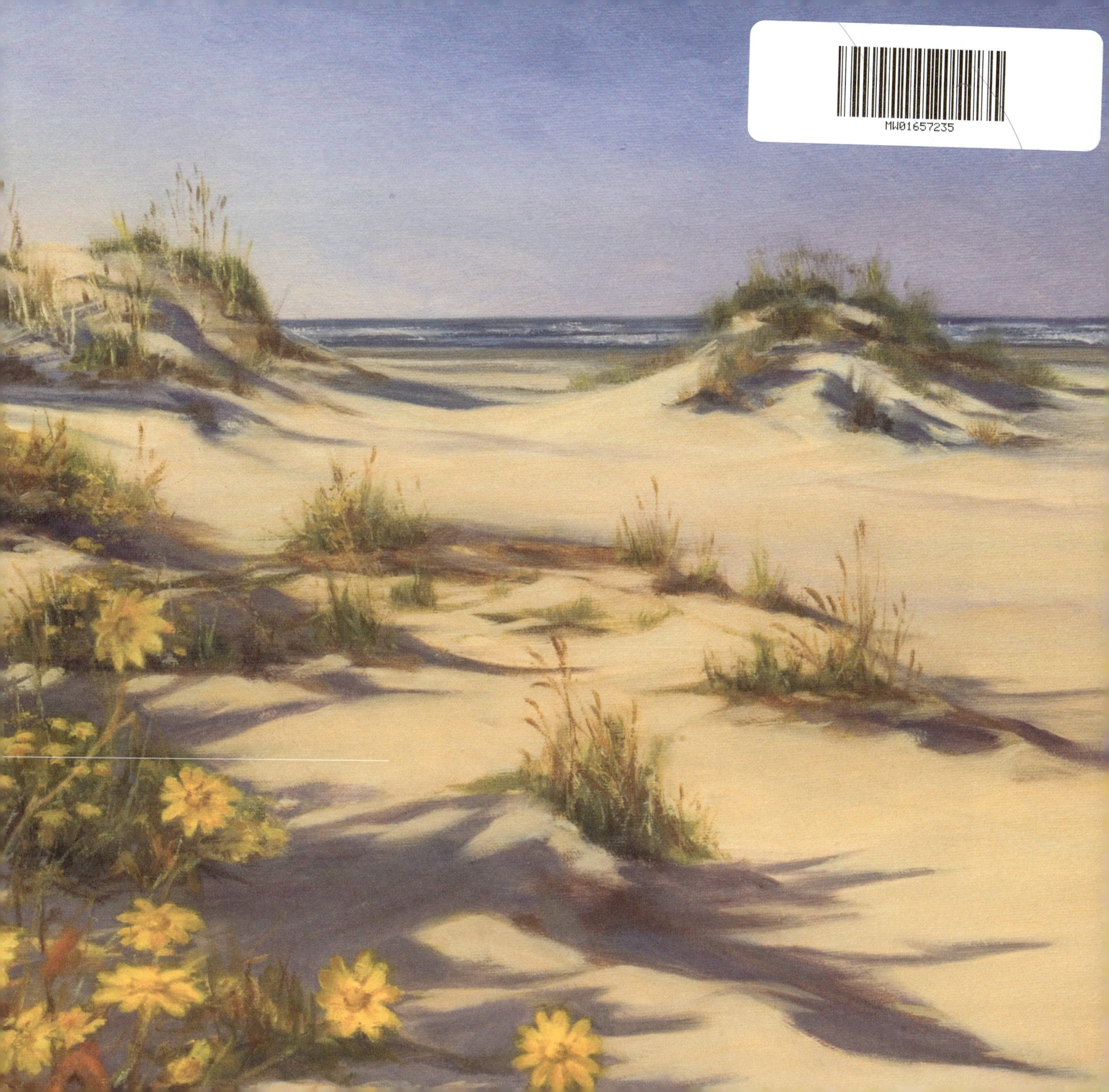

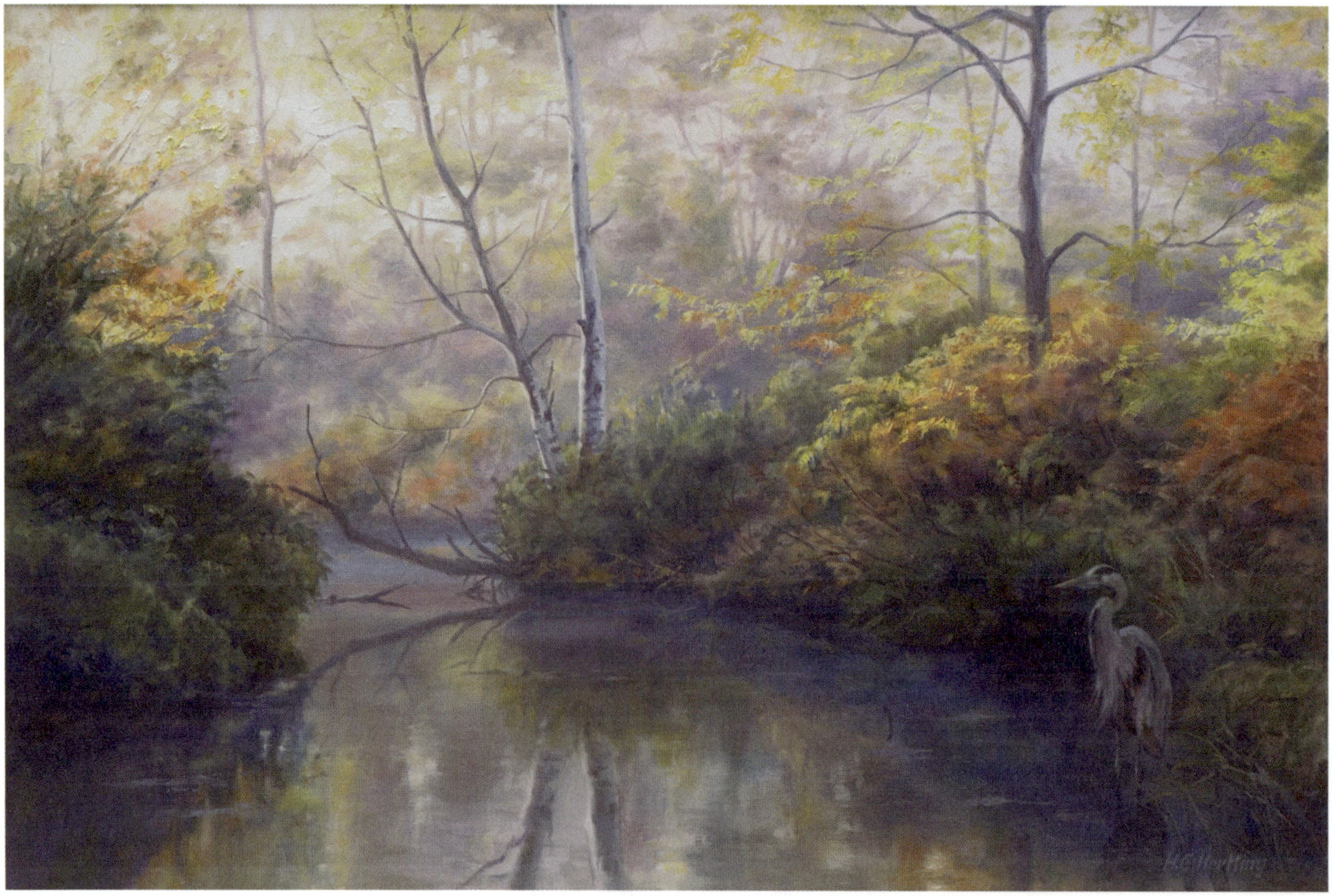

Autumn Palette, 22 x 30 Oil

Your Brush with Nature

by

Heiner C. Hertling

For everyone who ever said
"I can't paint!"

(But would really like to try)

Acknowledgements

I'd like to thank Carl Sams and Jean Stoick for their generosity with their time, equipment and helpful experience. Also thanks to Karen McDiarmid, my art director, designer, computer whiz, critic and guiding light throughout. Thanks to my wife Diane and my kids, especially Heidi for creative suggestions.

Thank you to my partners on the TV show *Your Brush With Nature,* David Tietmeyer and Jim Parkman. My appreciation goes to my painting buddies and students who asked for this book and to Christine Sarazin for pushing me to write it.

Inquiries about this book should be addressed to:

Heiner C. Hertling
P.O. Box 182
Milford, MI 48380
248/684-4371
germanart@aol.com
www.yourbrushwithnature.com www.heinerhertling.com

Hertling, Heiner C.
Your Brush With Nature: A Painting Guide for Everyone
by Heiner C. Hertling
H'Art Studios, Inc. © 2007

Summary: A painting guide for artists of all levels.

Printed and bound in Canada
Friesens of Altona, Manitoba

ISBN 13: 978-0-9795123-0-8

Painting Guide/Artists of all ages

Library of Congress Control Number: 2007903310

10 9 8 7 6 5 4 3 2 1

CONTENTS

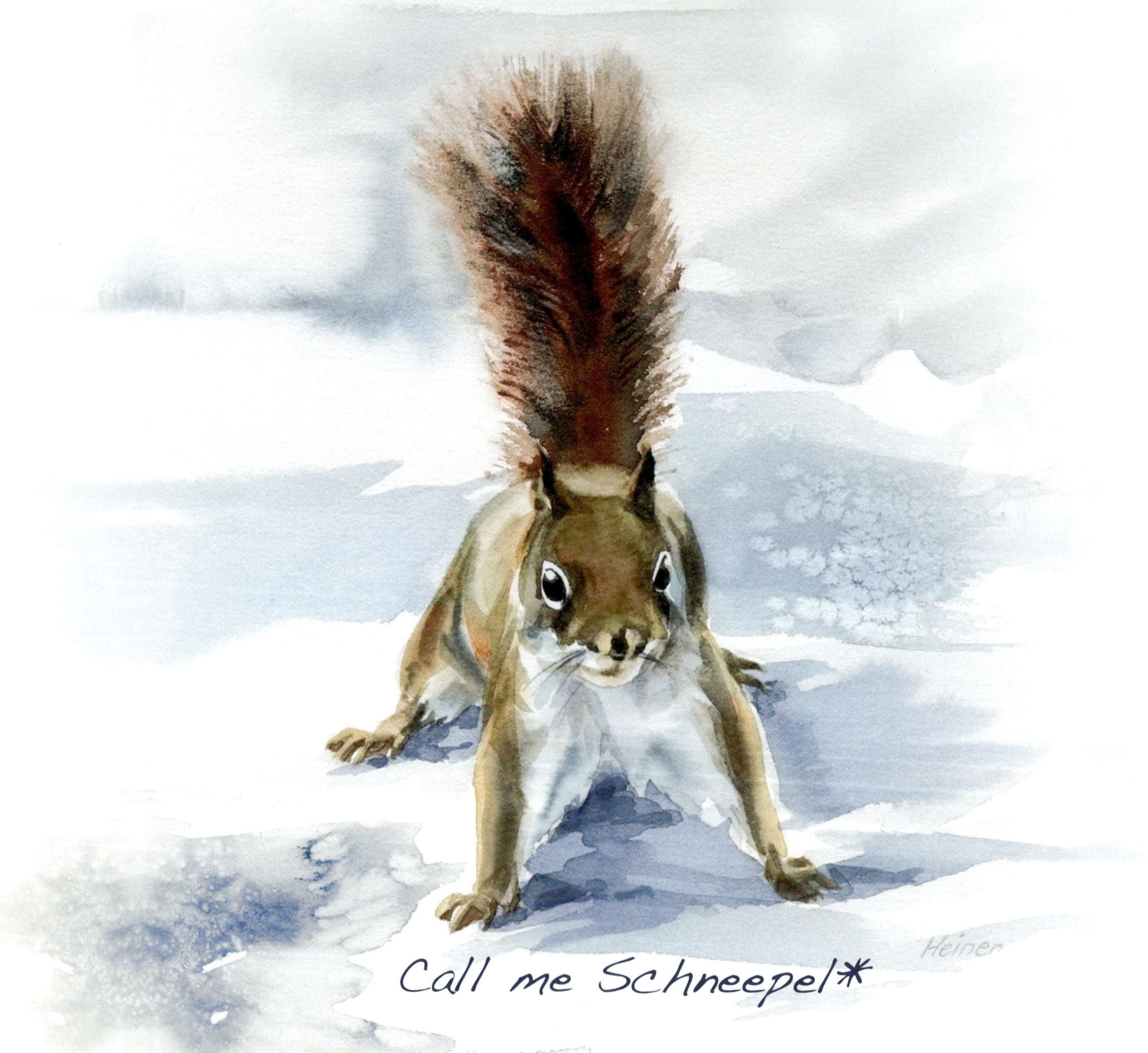

Call me Schneepel*

*Word origin is either Yiddish or German.
English equivalent is: what-cha-ma-call-it or thing-a-ma-jig!

INTRODUCTION

Oh yes, another art book! But hopefully with my little friend "Schneepel" we can keep you reading, looking and learning — even the younger artists.

Painting is creating something from beginning to end. The many different approaches and techniques of instructional journals have this idea in common. That is also my greatest joy in doing it. I love going from blank canvas, through excitement, trial and error, joy, frustration and discipline, to a finished painting. It feels like I've added something to the world that did not exist before. Art is a personal challenge. You open yourself up for praise or criticism. Most of the time it's like you are along for the ride while something is growing on the painting surface. Only after years and years of painting have I reached the point where I can see the finished piece in my mind from the very start— and not every time, even now. Before each new attempt I close my eyes and try to picture the finished painting.

Like any skill, good instruction is invaluable. Practice is important, too, as is the love for what you are doing. Talent in my opinion is overrated. It comes into play, but not as the number one requirement.

My love and appreciation for nature and the outdoors is the reason I most enjoy painting "plein aire" (French for painting outdoors in the open air). Even though this book is basically an oil painting guide, all other media are involved because the basics are often the same (design, values, color, edges, etc.). As always, my little friend Schneepel had to be different and insisted on being painted in watercolor.

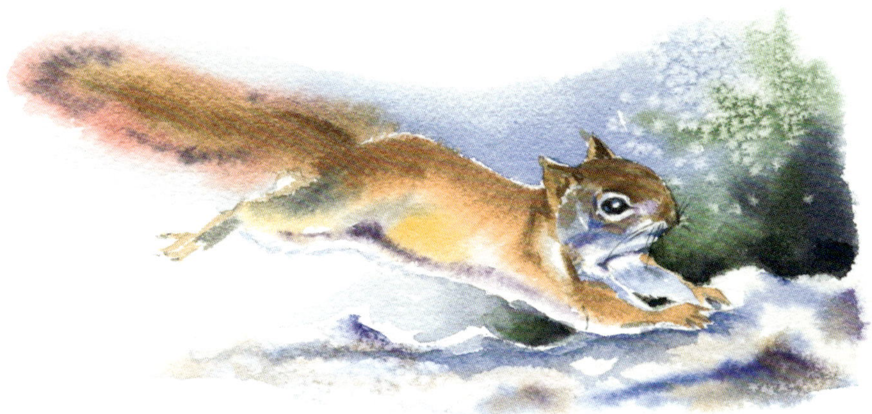

I am fast – LIKE WATERCOLOR PAINTING!

BENEFITS

The fantastic benefits of painting are numerous! There is no age limit in either direction, you can preserve memories from beautiful locations, create inexpensive presents for family and friends and learn to look at the world more carefully. You will learn to study a subject intently and challenge yourself to get better all the time. It's a chance to take a break from the daily chase after the almighty dollar. The freedom to do exactly what you want is great. In my case, not working in commercial art for some art director feels good.

There is permanence to a painting. A beautiful dance or musical performance (if not recorded) disappears into space to say nothing of an ice sculpture. Camaraderie with fellow painters is great. So is travel to beautiful places to view and paint. Challenging yourself to master a new skill is rewarding.

I want to share with you the experiences and knowledge I've accumulated over a half a century.

Follow Schneepel and me through the next pages and when you get to the end, start over again.
IT WILL SINK IN!

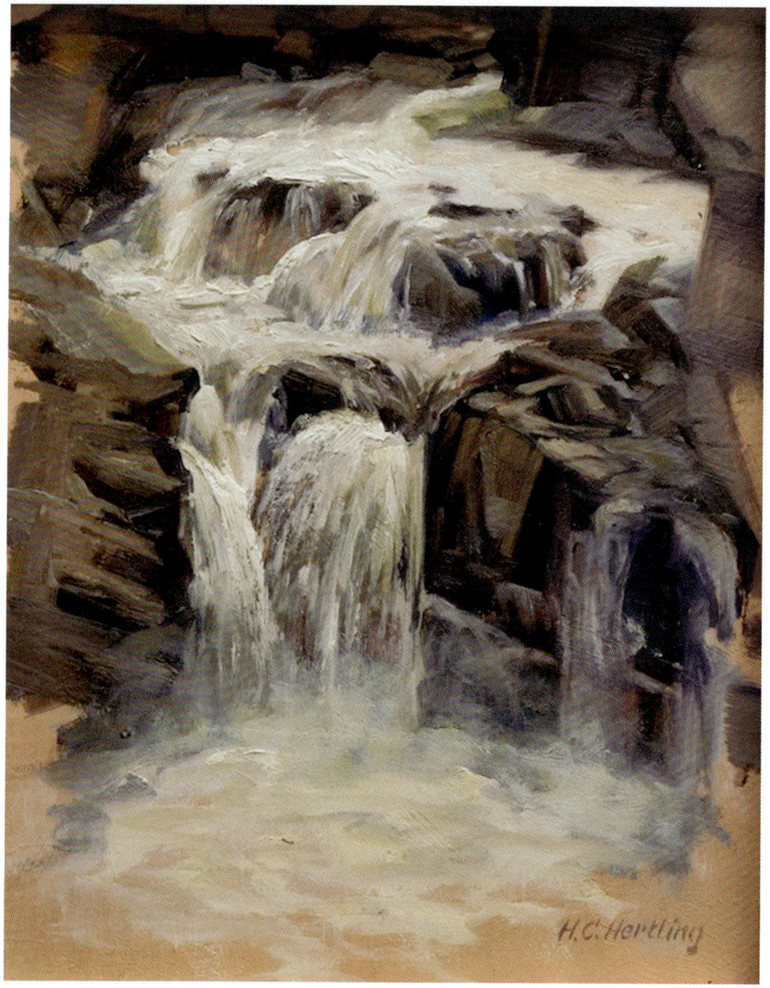

Many Glacier, Glacier National Park, 9 x 12 Oil

MATERIALS

1. *The painting surface:* hardboard (Masonite), canvas boards and canvases. If you stretch your own canvases to make unconventional sizes, you will need to have a staple gun, stretcher bars and stretcher pliers.

2. *Brushes:* It is very important to have good brushes. I use no more than five different types and sizes: large flat or bright (#12), medium flat or bright (#8), medium filbert (#8), small flat or bright (#4) and pointed small round (#2). If you can find them with black ferrels instead of chrome, you won't get sunlight flashed into your eyes or onto your work.

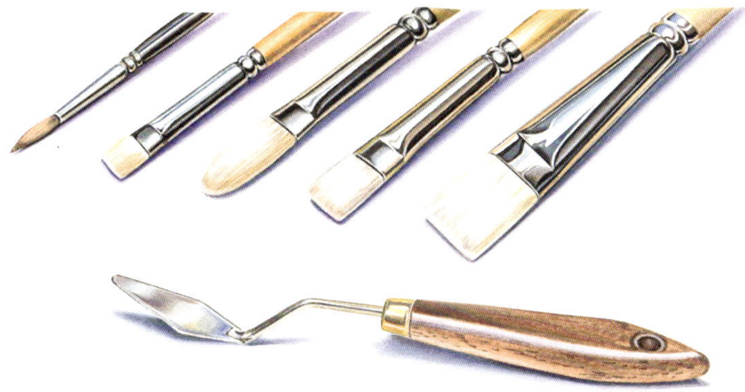

Schneepel thinks that the guy who invented chrome on brushes never painted outdoors.

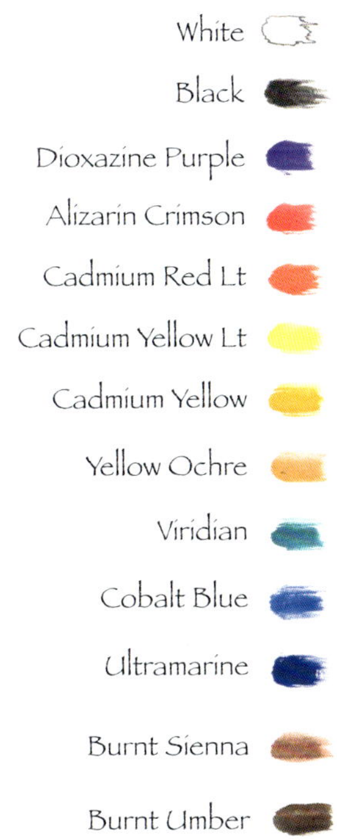

3. *Palette knives:* two sizes — 1" and 2" offset handle pointed type.

4. *Paint:* I use about 12 colors. I like Graham walnut oil based paint as shown and you certainly can add to this assortment if you like.

5. *Painting medium (thinner):* Outdoors I don't mind mineral spirits but indoors, I use oil (walnut oil) or even other vegetable oils and my studio smells a lot better. For health reasons, stay away from turpentine. Liquin can be added to the paint to make it dry faster.

6. *Easels:* Indoors — large and permanent. Outdoors — light and sturdy.

7. *For painting outdoors* think about having a view finder, a malstick to steady your hand, rags in a box (auto supply store), hand cleaner and a wet painting carrier. In cold weather add long underwear, Carharts, hand warmers, fingerless gloves, hat and boots. If you have one, carry a painting umbrella. Don't wear a brightly colored shirt as it reflects onto your canvas.

PREPARATION

Before you start painting, I want you to do the following:

1. *Prepare your painting surface:* If you prime your own boards or canvases, you need gesso (acrylic underpaint). If you're using Masonite, rough up the top surface a little with sandpaper, coat both sides with the gesso to prevent warping. The side to be painted should receive a second coat with a bit of texture added. I use an old house paintbrush or a palette knife to create the texture. Now here's a helpful time saving tip: Mix an acrylic earthtone such as burnt sienna with your white gesso to create a warm undertone instead of bright white. If you start with a primed canvas, wipe a thin burnt sienna mix onto the surface and even it out with paper towel or rags. If you don't like the absorbent, even chalky surface of gesso, just spray the board with a little bit of damar varnish. It closes the pores and the paint glides easier.

2. *Get yourself a sketchbook:* Here you can do all your thinking with a pencil. For example, do you want to do this painting horizontally or vertically? Make thumbnail sketches. Thumbnails are quick little doodles like this:

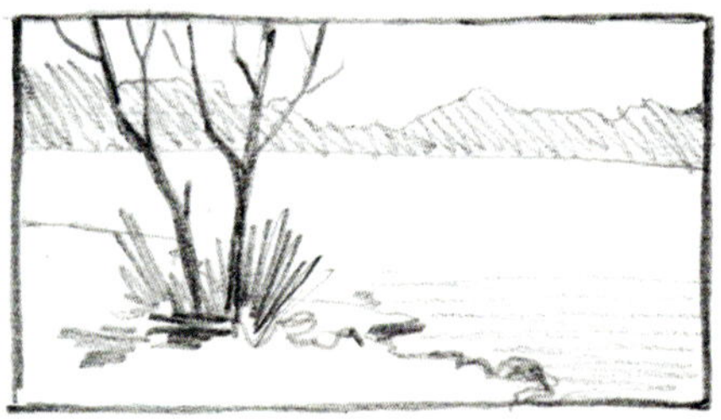

Yes! Horizontal

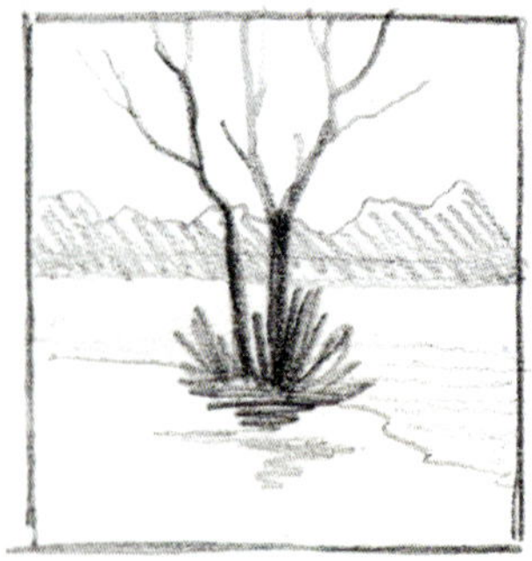

too centered

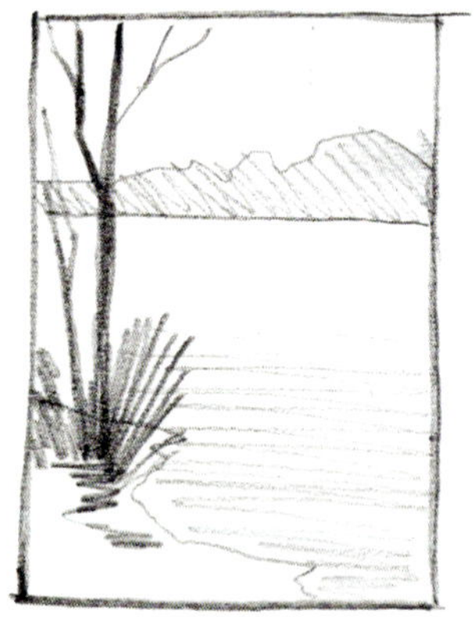

crowded

Don't use the outer edges of the paper as your frame. Instead make little pencil rectangles in the proportion of your canvas or board. They only have to be a few inches in size. You can indicate the main masses of your image, block in the darkest dark and think about your focal point. Doing this will eliminate mistakes that could become a major headache when you are painting. You can also note the date, conditions, locations and so on. It is fun to go back later and remember that day. Buyers often want to know more about the painting they purchased.

Just wait! You will sell one sooner or later!

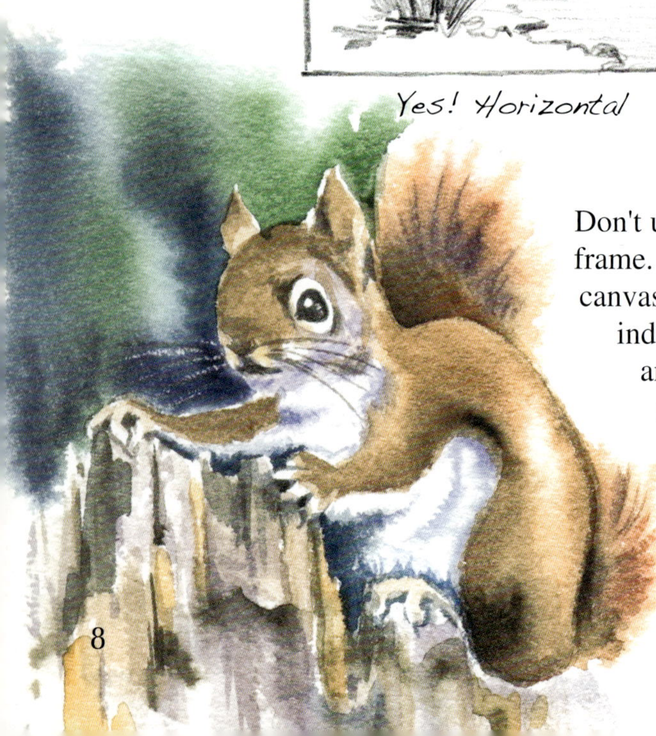

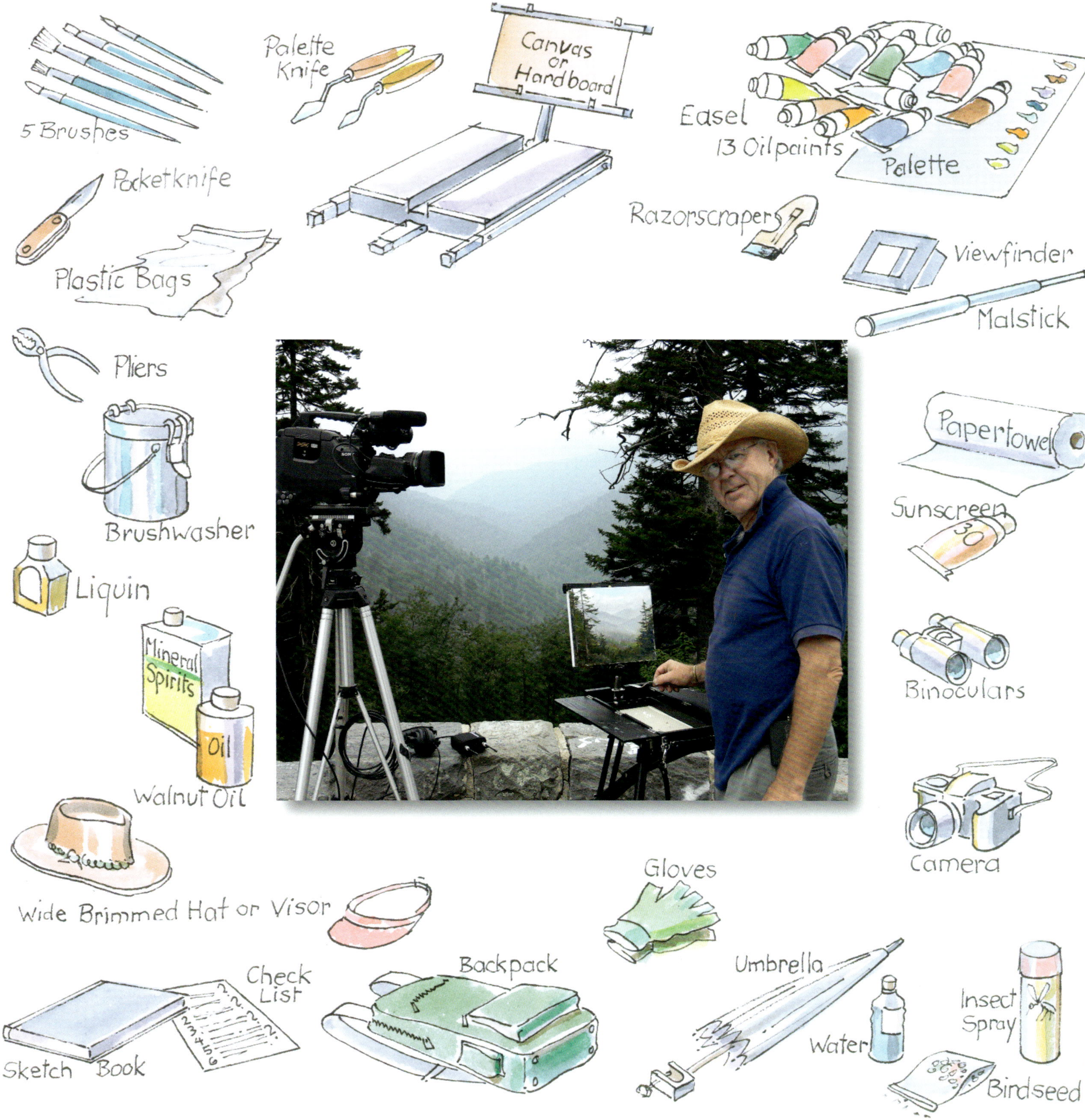
5 Brushes
Palette Knife
Canvas or Handboard
Easel
13 Oilpaints
Palette
Pocketknife
Plastic Bags
Razorscrapers
Viewfinder
Malstick
Pliers
Papertowel
Brushwasher
Sunscreen
30
Liquin
Mineral Spirits
Oil
Walnut Oil
Binoculars
Camera
Wide Brimmed Hat or Visor
Gloves
Check List
Backpack
Umbrella
Insect Spray
Water
Sketch Book
Birdseed

TECHNIQUES

Before we start our first paint-along demo let's do this exercise:

Brushes

A large brush will lay down a good amount of paint quickly and should be used a lot especially in plein air painting. The edges of flat brushes, either square or filbert, can be used to make amazingly fine lines. Try pulling or pushing your brush to get different effects. Small round sables are great for detail. One rule for all these brushes is not to hold them too tightly. It is not a pencil so move your hand back on the handle. I sometimes drop my brush because I hold it so delicately. The small round brush, which I use to do branches or like objects, is held by the very end of the handle and twisted while making the stroke.

When looking at a very detailed painting, people often think you had to use a brush with one hair. Wrong. One hair would not hold enough paint. A good pointed sable #3 brush holds paint and comes to a great point. As I have said before, good quality brushes are important and make your work easier.

Palette

Let's do another exercise using our palette knife. First find a clean, flat spot on your palette, mix the color you want to apply to your canvas and create a thin even layer of paint. Then touch an edge of your knife into it. You should have an even amount of paint along the edge. Touch the edge to your painting and create straight lines, grasses or any thin line you need.

I like to use the knife a lot, especially for more detail in grasses, cattails, or rigging on boats. Also straight edges on architectural structures are easily done with the knife. When used in combination with brushes, it is one of the most helpful tools. Since we don't want to show only one technique, be careful not to over use it. I know it's fun to use, but try to concentrate on capturing your subject without making the viewer see only your knife technique.

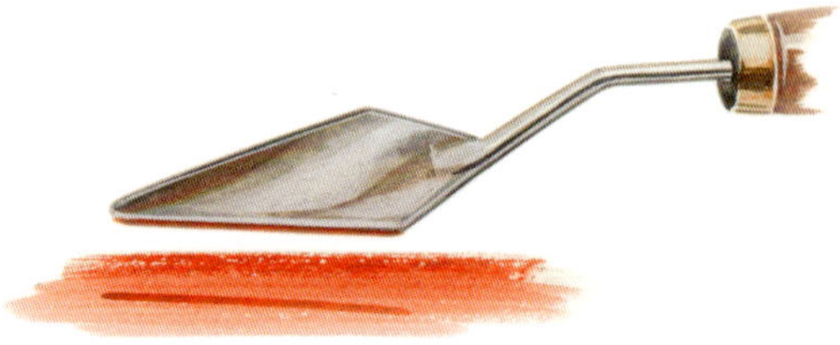

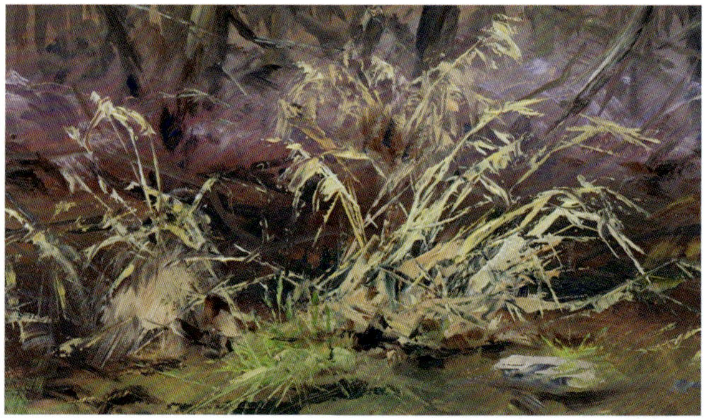

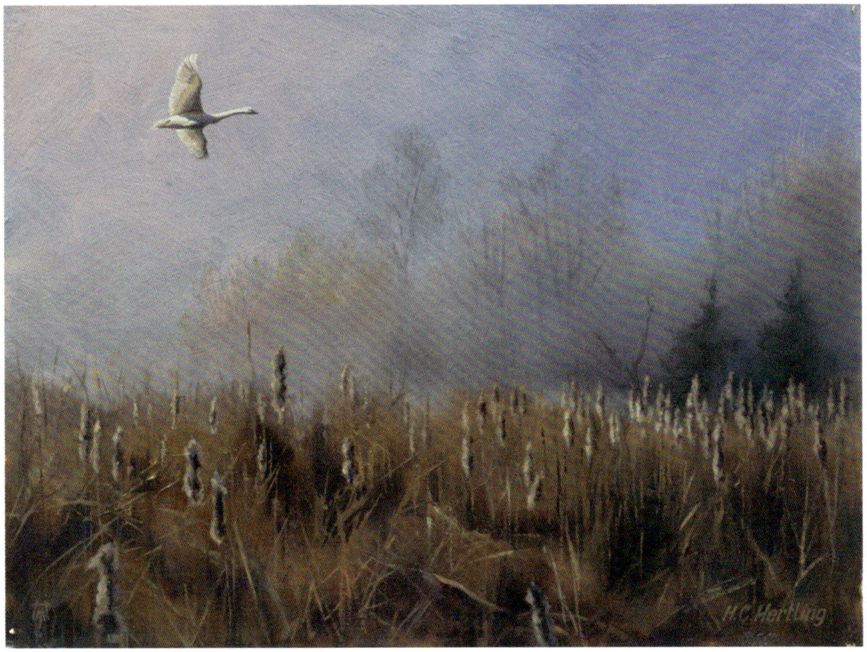

Flying Solo, 18 x 24 Oil

I created the thin stems and seed heads with my knife first. Then I softened them with a big brush. A small sable round brush added the curved grasses. Using all your tools in combination is the trick.

All the thin cables in riggings on boats are created with the edge of my knife. I also use it for sharp edges wherever needed.

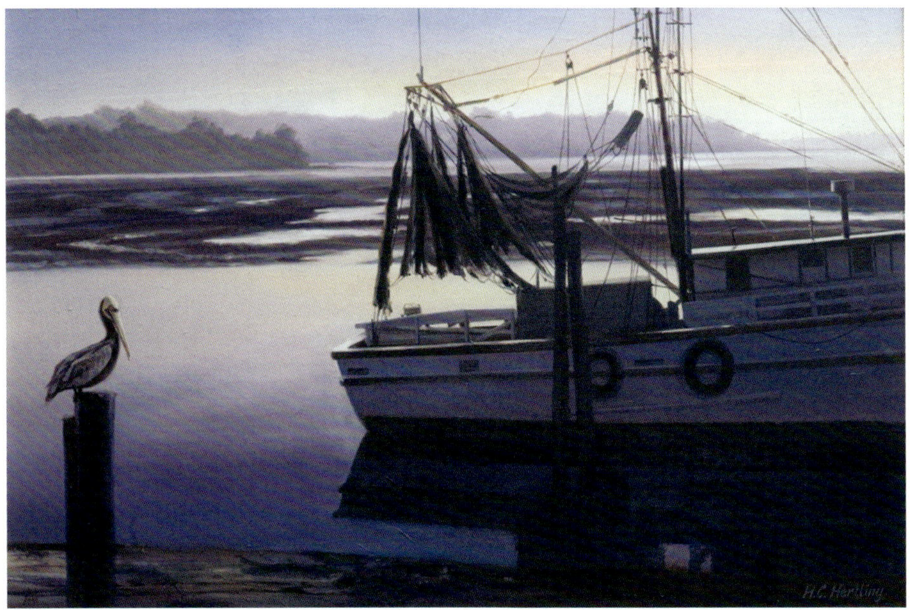

Day is Done, 18 x 26 Oil

STEP-BY-STEP

First paint-along demo

Use a 9″ x 12″ or 11″ x 14″ surface. Those sizes are big enough. If you think you can't draw well, pick something that doesn't require difficult skills like drawing perspective, ellipses, straight lines and so on. Sometimes a pleasant uncomplicated landscape can be a very good start. Also spend time learning to draw. Read books, take lessons and practice.

For your first efforts, I recommend staying in the studio (basement, kitchen or guest room). The conditions outdoors add too many distractions and we don't need that yet.

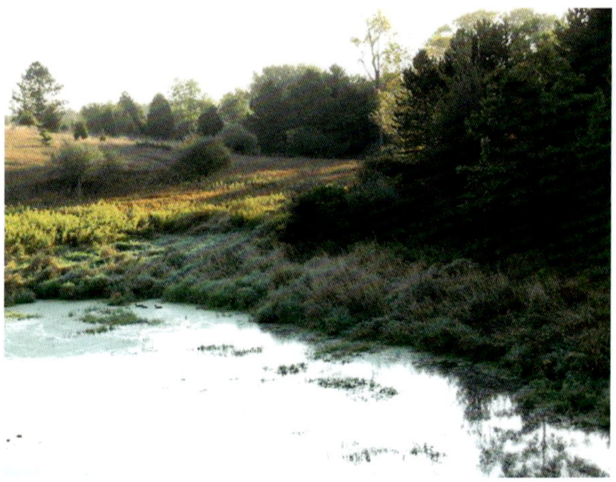

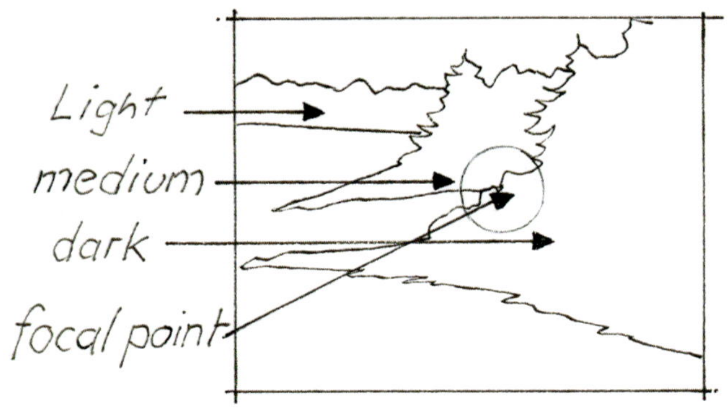

Pick a pleasant picture that you always thought would make a pretty painting. I have picked mine and in the following demo steps I will help you make a "game plan". This game plan is very important and should be followed from the beginning to the end. It simplifies the process of painting but requires the most thinking.

Ask yourself these questions. Where is my focal point? Where is the darkest dark and lightest light? Where is the light source? A focal point is an area in your painting where you want the viewer's eye to go first. Achieve this by knowing the following facts:

1. Your eyes almost always go to the place where the darkest dark and the lightest light meet with a fairly hard edge.
2. The brightest colors attract your eyes as well.
3. Your eyes also go to the most detailed area.
4. Leading lines will direct your eyes to the focal point.

HOW DO WE START?

Let's draw the main shapes, either with a pencil or little brush loaded with a thinned out earthtone. Ignore detail in your reference and try to break the whole image, in this case, into five large shapes.

Make sure your brushes, thinner and palette are clean because even the smallest amount of light color robs the darks (like cobalt blue, dioxazine purple, burnt umber, alizarin crimson) of their intensity. If there is a dark shape in the foreground block it in now (5). You might not touch that area again until the end of the painting.

Next I like to start with the most distant shape (1).

We want to create a 3-dimensional image on a 2-dimensional board. That's a challenge. But have no fear, there are ways. What did you see when you looked at mountains far off in the distance? Remember how light, blue and flat they appeared? Well that is one way to create the illusion of distance. They have to be lighter, often bluer and have no razor sharp edges (with my eyesight that's easy).

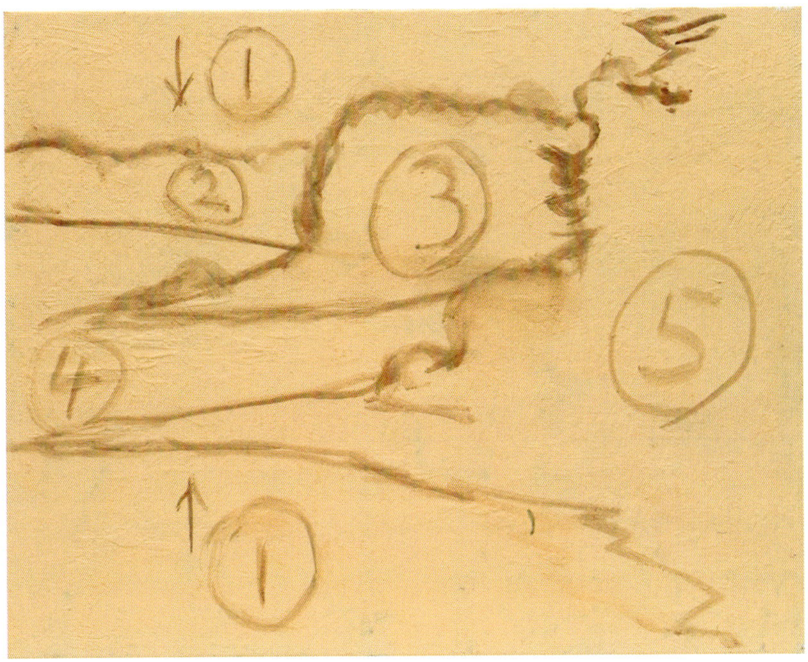

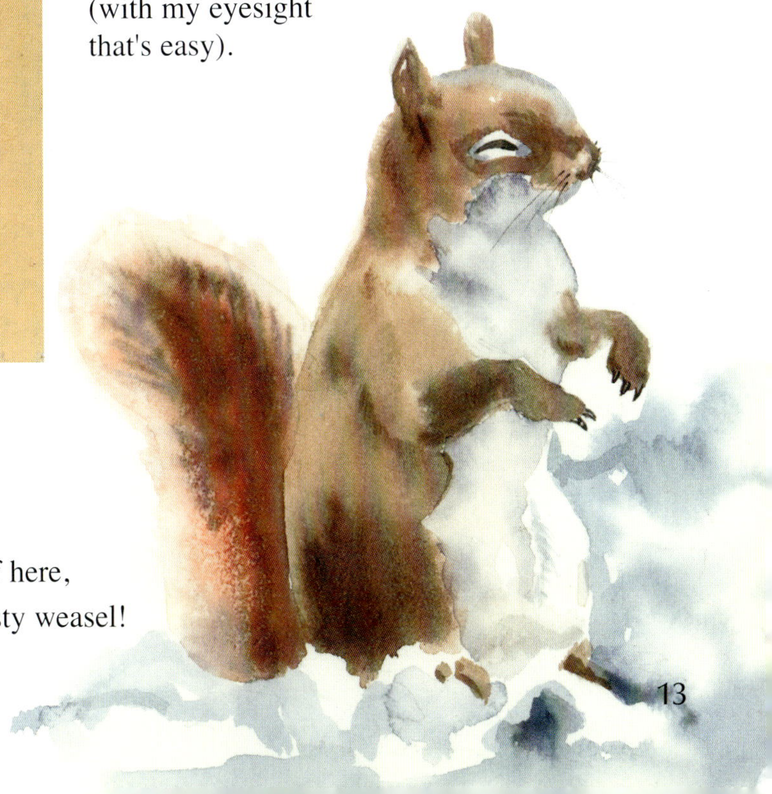

Schneepel! Get out of here,
you nasty weasel!

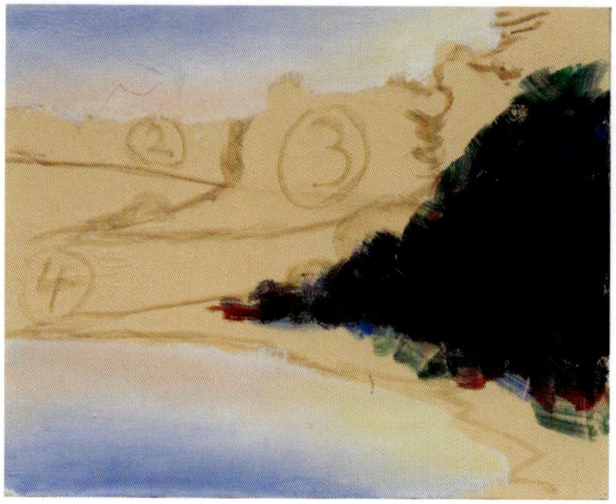

Let's get back to the steps. The sky is the most distant part on the canvas (1). I lay some white all over the sky area. Then depending upon the time of day, season or mood you want to add the sky color from the top down. Make it darker on the top and lighter to the horizon line. It gives you a cove effect instead of a flat wall. It's the opposite in the water reflection.

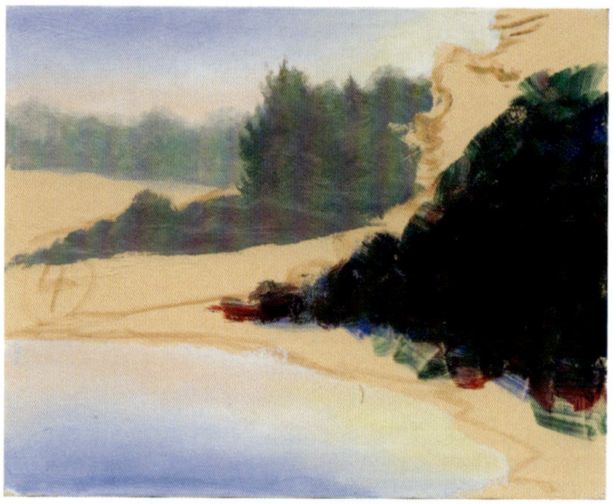

Now the next distant shape is the tree line or mountains. (2) Squint (partially close your eyes) at your reference and think about the dominant color. Paint that shape but keep it fairly light to create the distance(3). When you start painting that part you only have to pay attention to the upper edge where it overlaps the sky. The bottom edge will be covered by the next shape.

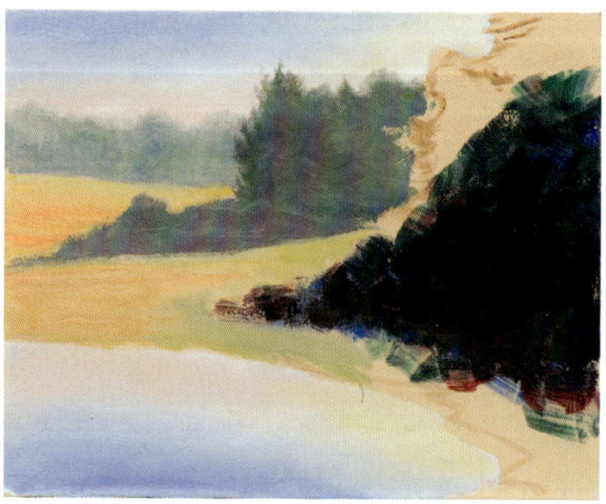

The next shape (4) the ground and grasses, get a little brighter in color and the edges can be a little sharper.

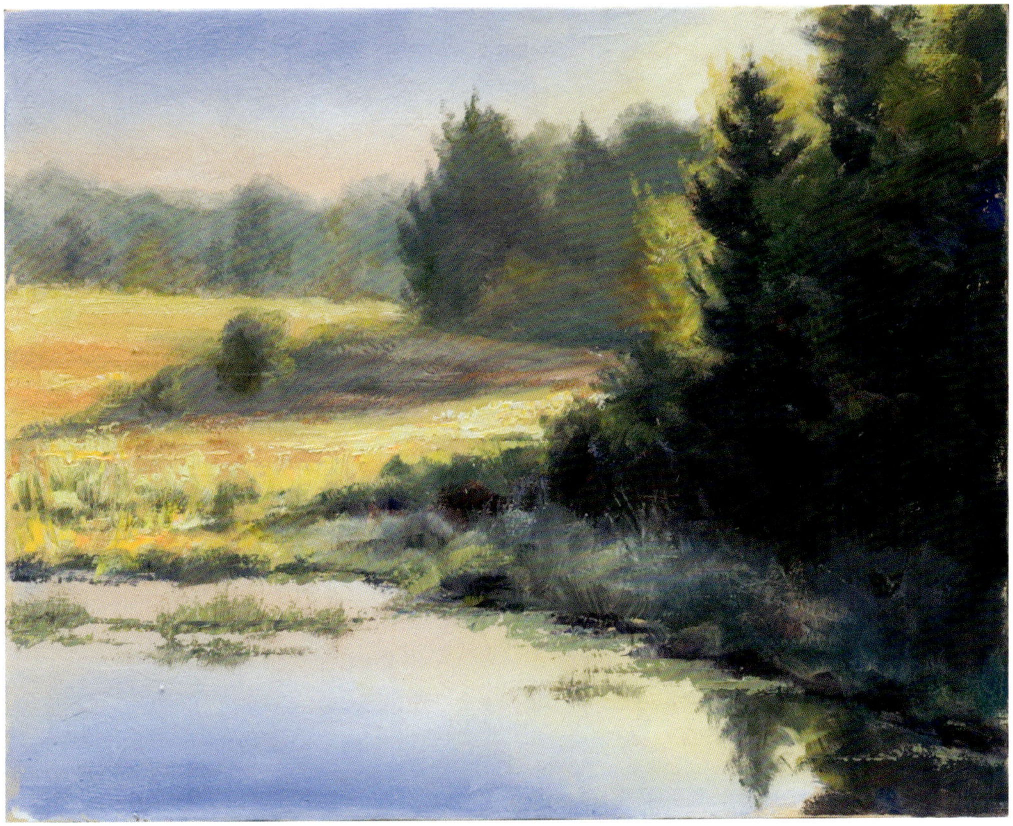

My Secret Pond, 11 x 14 Oil Finished Painting

When you have filled in your five shapes with the correct dominating color, you can think about adding more detail. Finish the edges (trees, grasses, etc.) by studying the characteristic shapes. Sometimes we have to forget what we learned when we were little. A pine tree is not always the triangular Christmas tree, and other trees are not always round on top, with green leaves and a brown trunk. Look, look and look again! The light falling on subjects does change the appearance of things and that light is what we want to paint. Shadows do the same thing and cannot be ignored.

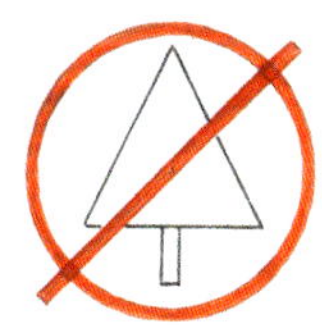

In oil painting you can add or subtract (wipe off) color for quite awhile. Often I find myself mixing my colors on the canvas instead of on the palette. By not completely blending those colors you create "broken color", meaning the whole spectrum is present. A green forest is full of different colors such as browns, blues, yellows and oranges, not just greens.

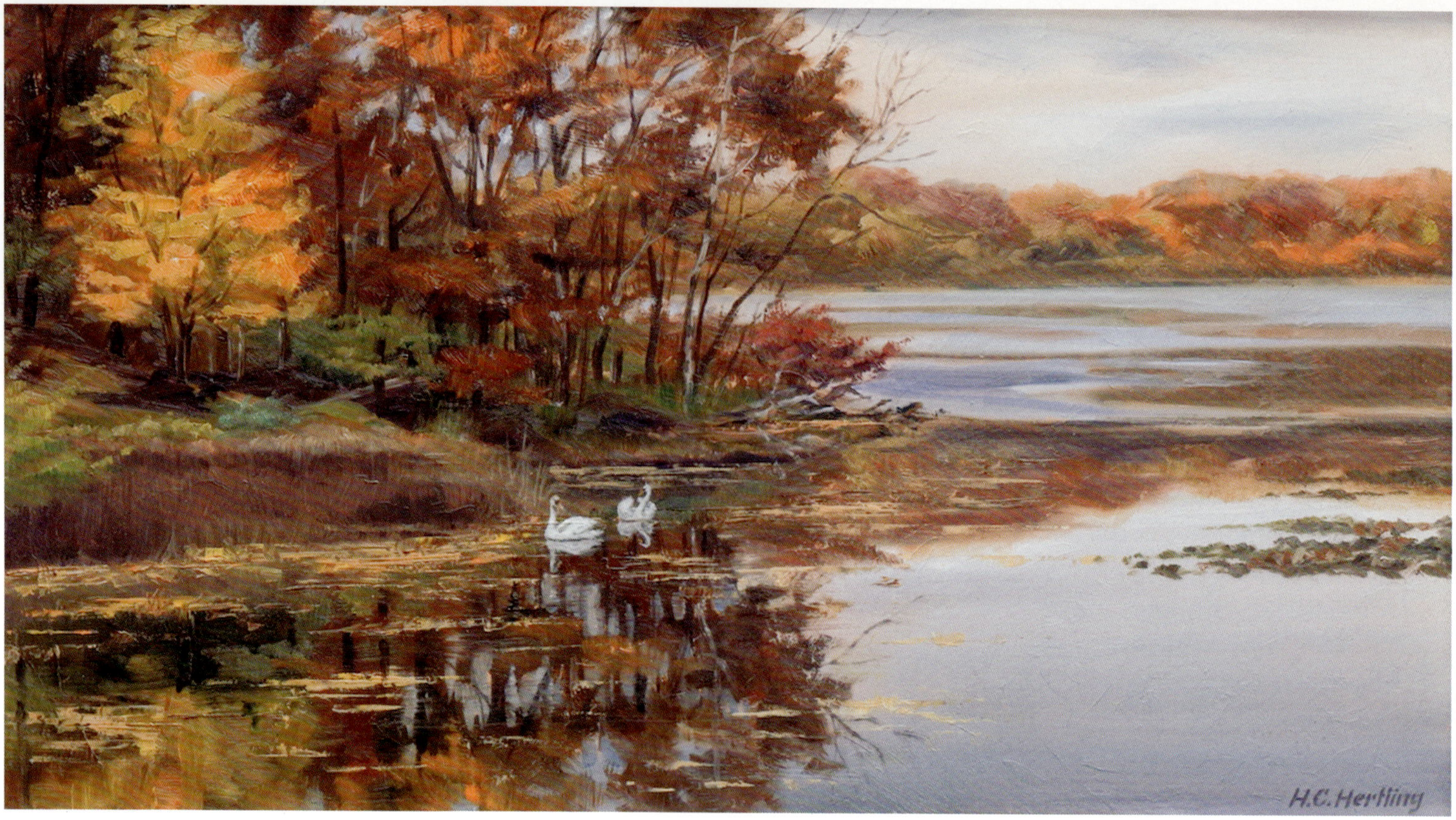

Wild Wing Lake, 12 x 24 Oil

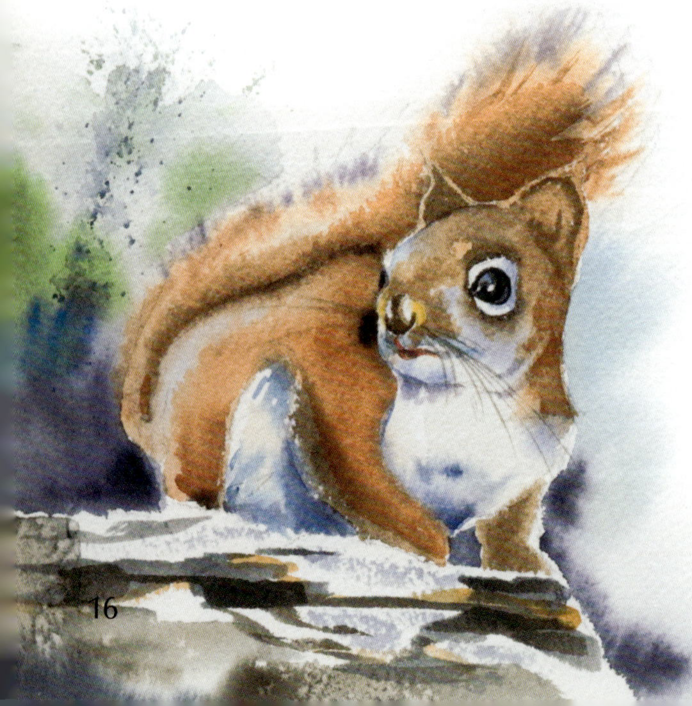

In an impressionistic painting, you don't want to get carried away with too much detail. For example, if you are painting a tree it is not necessary to paint each individual leaf even if there are thousands. It is the larger shape that you must capture, then it will look like you have painted one thousand leaves. Spell out a few more detailed leaves on the edges and, voila, oak leaves. To finish the piece, look at page 33 for some negative painting tips.

I think that people who are fascinated with detail often don't understand the difference between painting and photography. Besides, I only counted 999 leaves in that painting!

Well, he can be harsh like that. He is right though. Once you proved you could do 10 nice leaves, what does one thousand prove? Patience? Instead, spend your time studying other aspects of drawing or painting.

Let's throw him a few nuts and quiet him down.

GALLERY

The humidity of early morning was a challenge to paint.

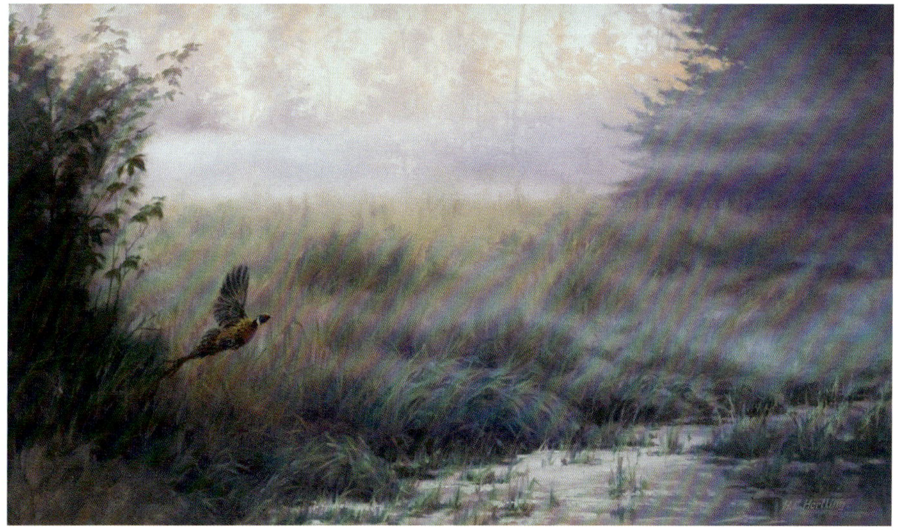

Into the Mist, 24 x 32 Oil

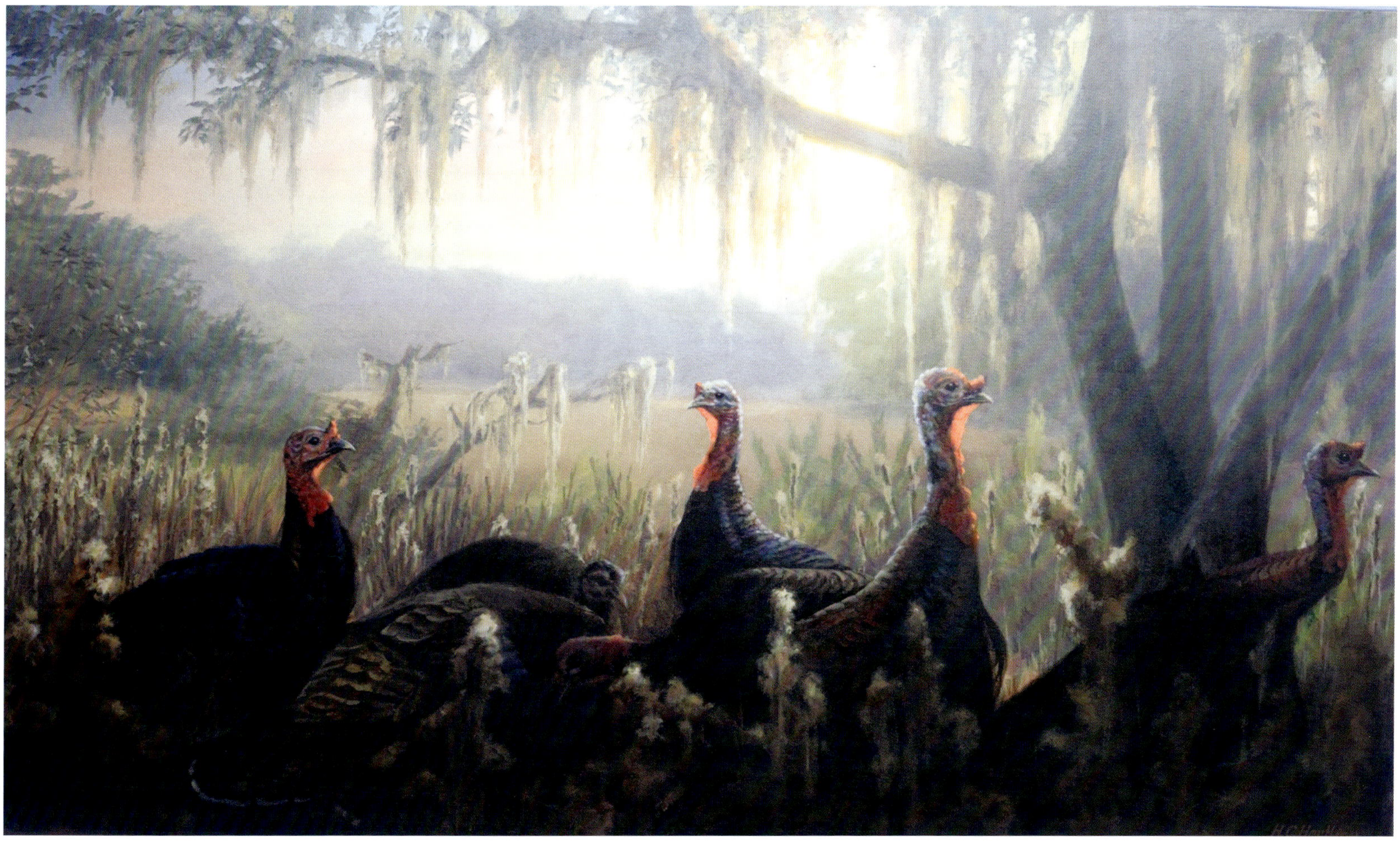

Southern Sunrise, 32 x 48 Oil

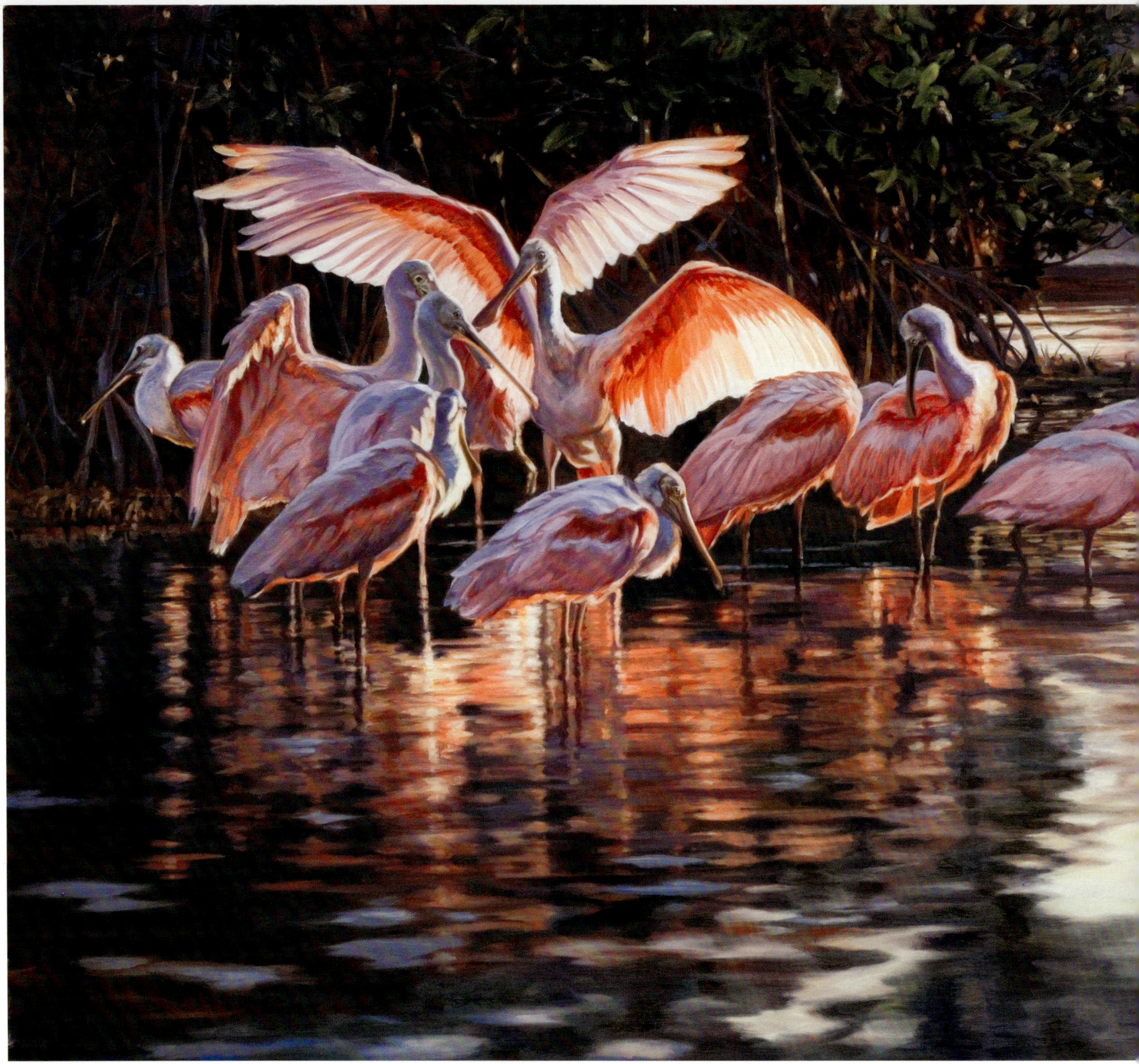

Roseate Spoonbills   J.N. “Ding” Darling National Wildlife Refuge, Sanibel Island, Florida

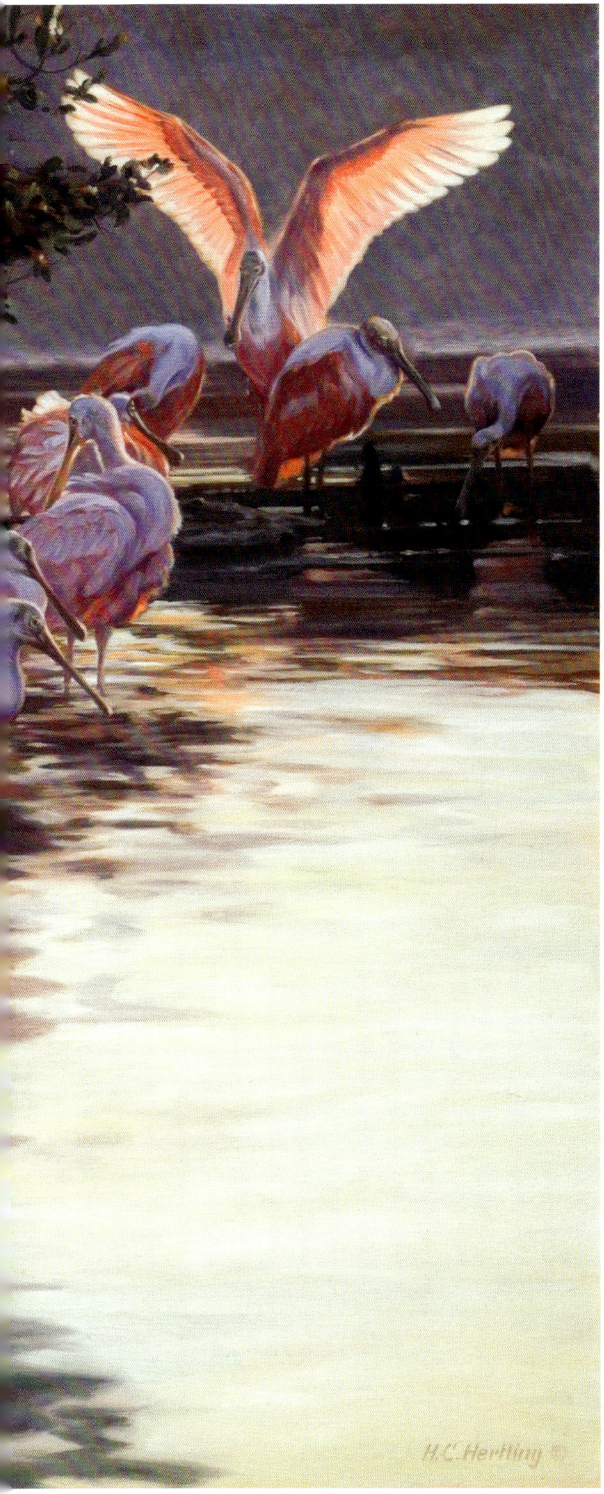

Happy Hour, 32 x 48 Oil

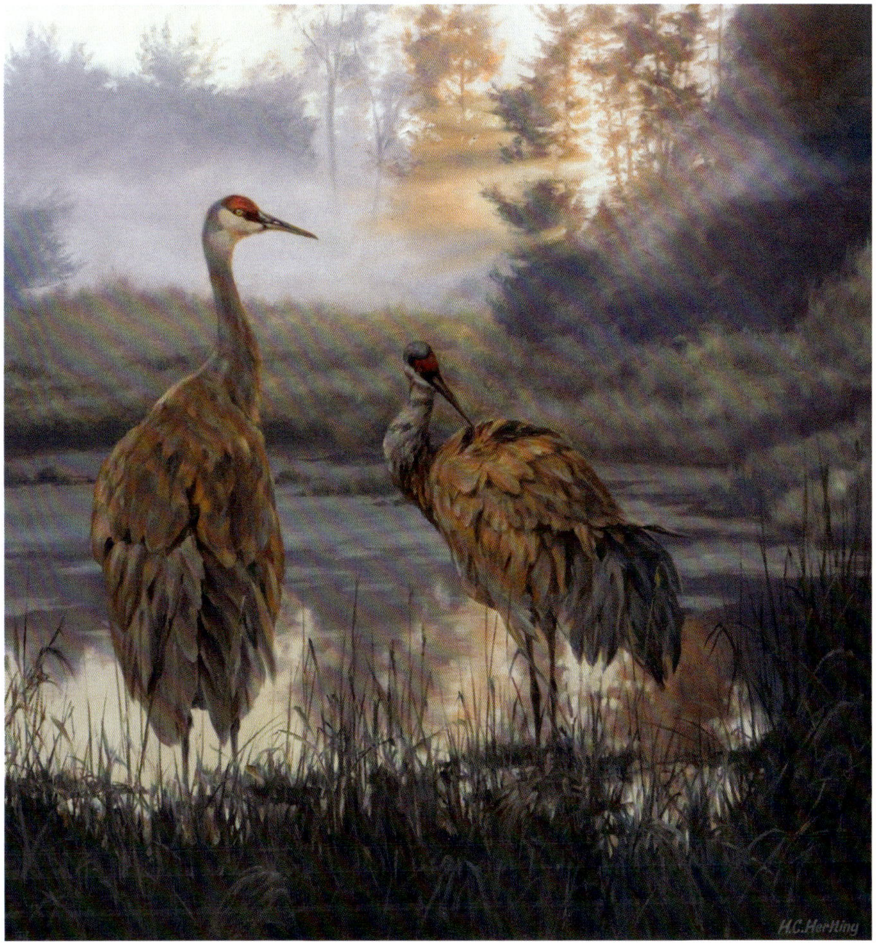

Sandhill Cranes   Michigan in September   Morning Light, 28 x 30 Oil

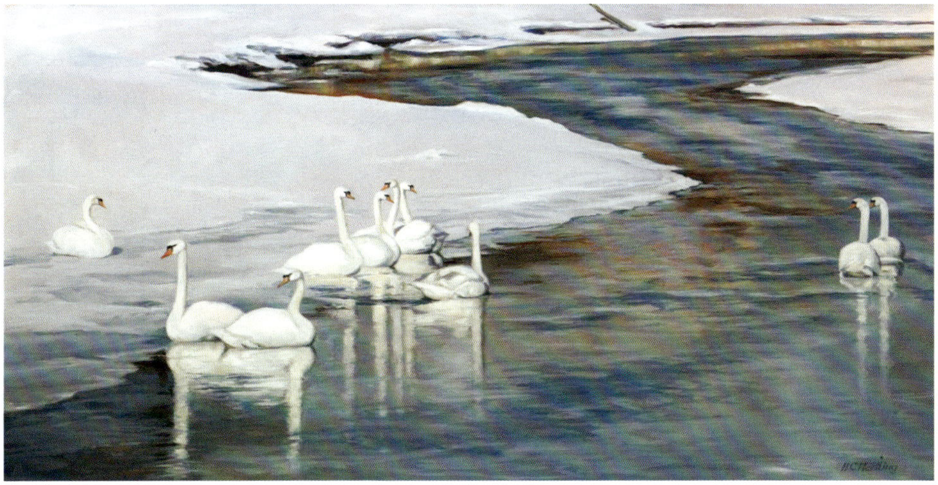

Mute Swans   Huron River   White on White, 24 x 48 Oil

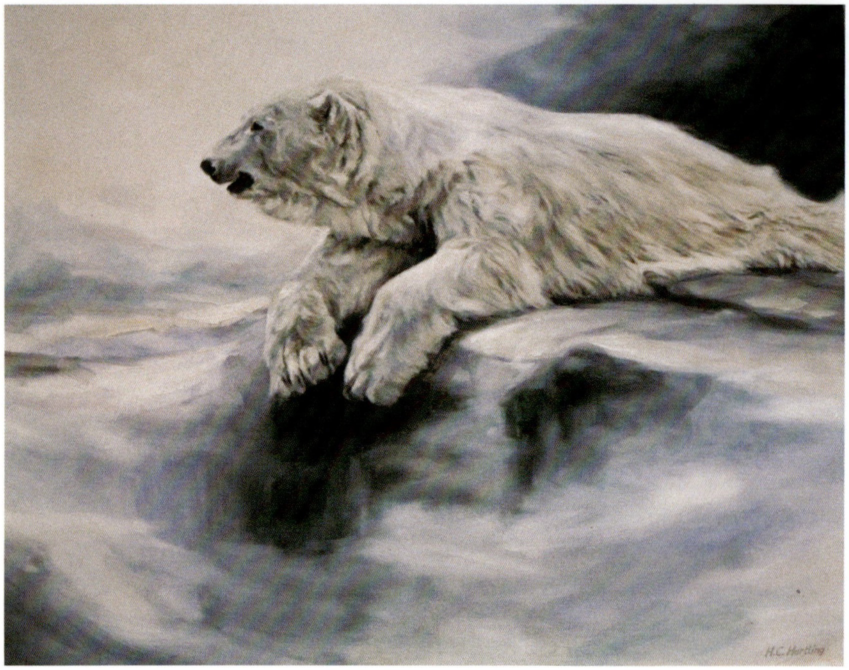

Ice Bear, 32 x 42 Oil

The reference for this painting is from the zoo in my native Hamburg, Germany.

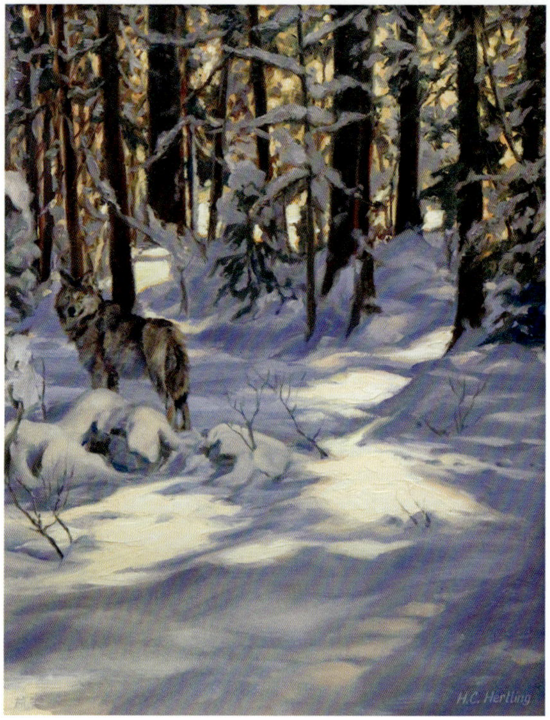

Sunspots, 16 x 20 Oil

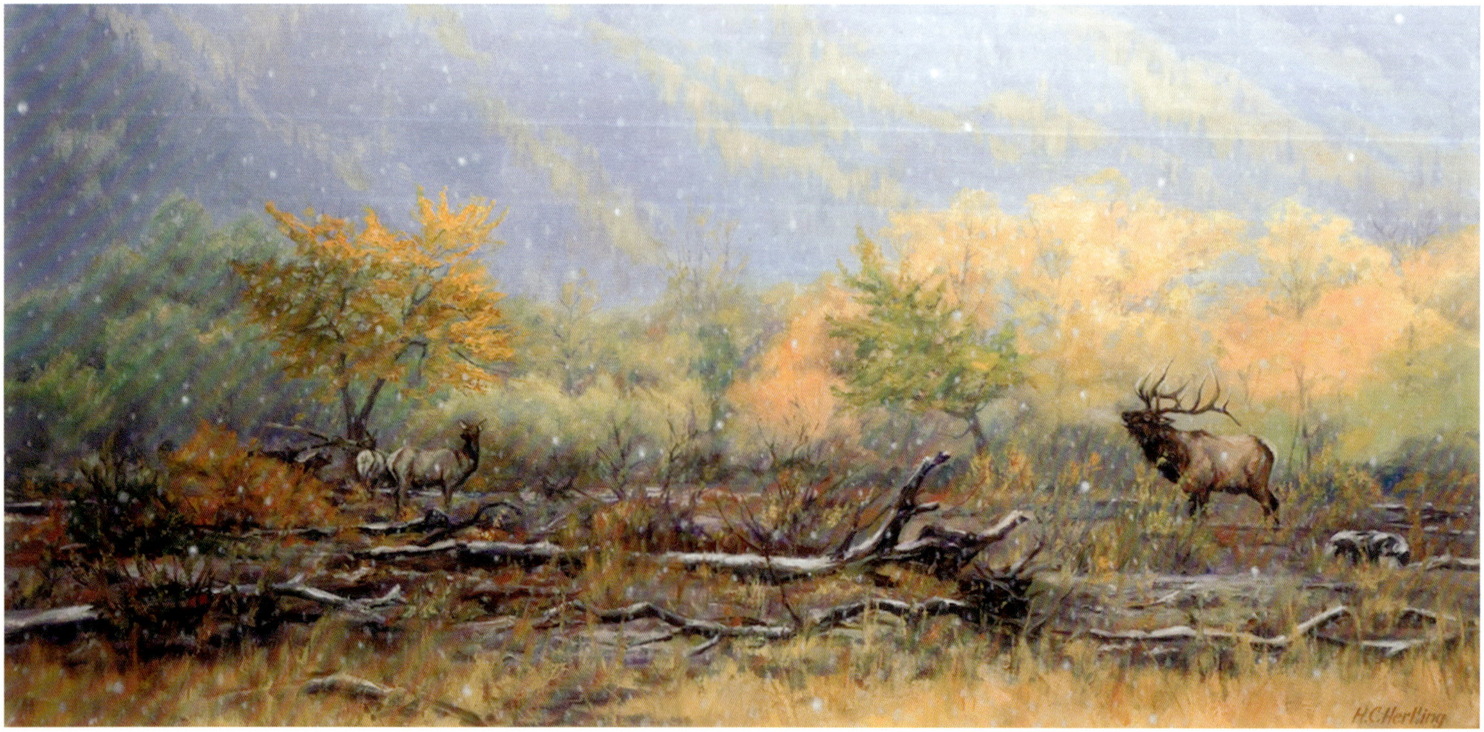

Returning the Call, 24 x 48 Oil

First Snow in Waterton Lakes National Park, Alberta, Canada

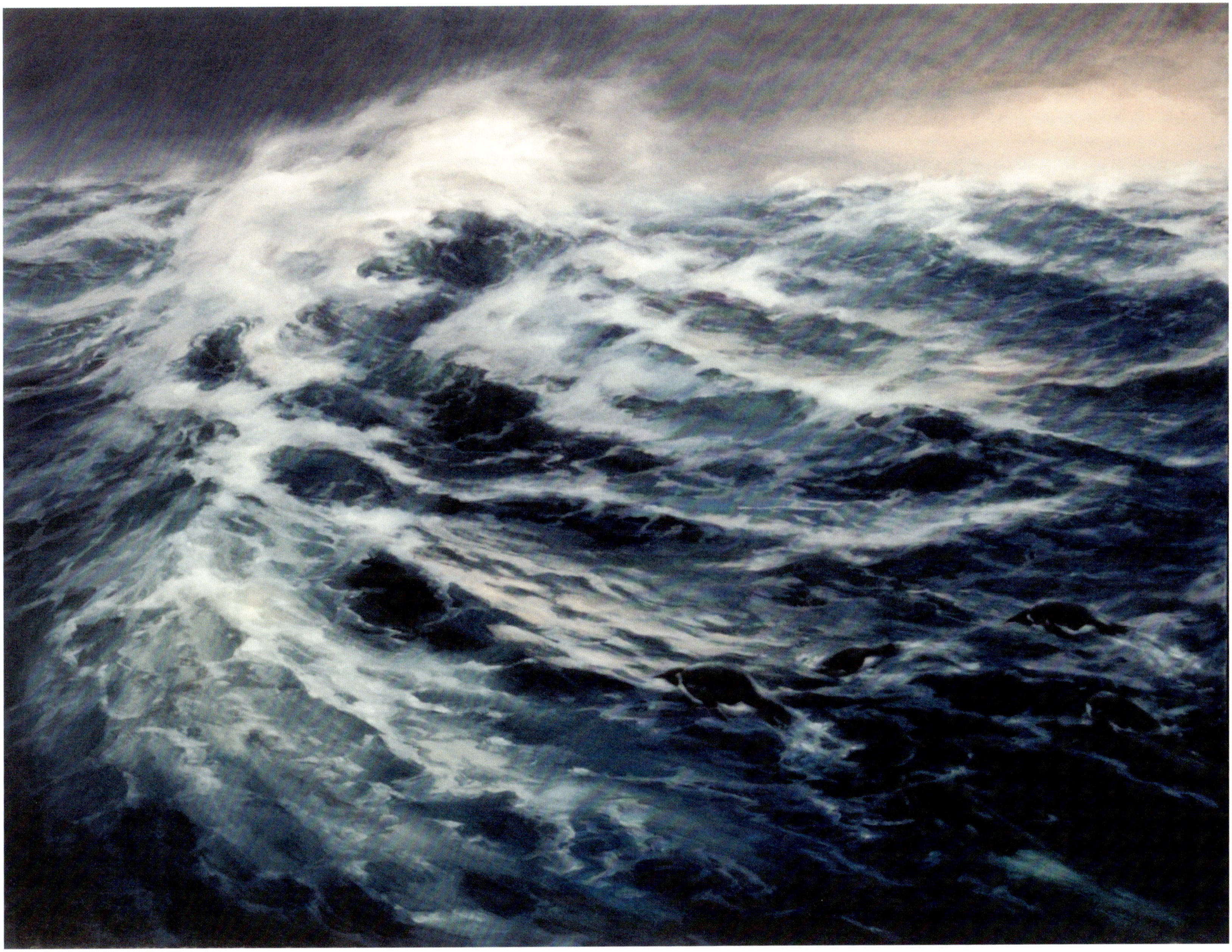

These penguins going out to the fishing ground were a figment of my imagination.

Rhythm in Blues, 30 x 48 Oil

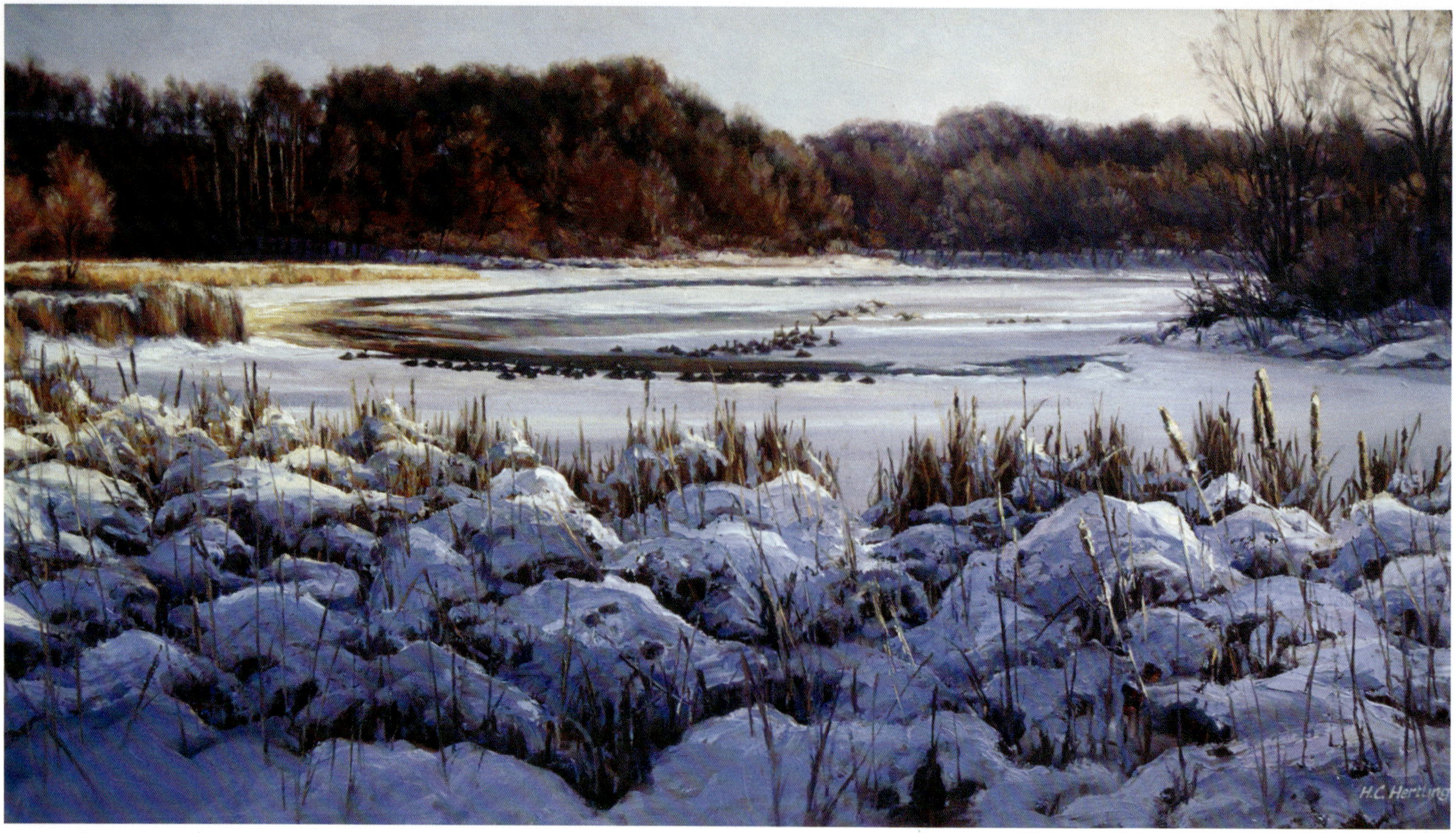

Huron River Cattails, 28 x 46 Oil *The last open water on the Huron attracted the birds, the snow covered cattails attracted me.*

Pelicans soaring over the dunes in Carolina added life to this very simple scene.

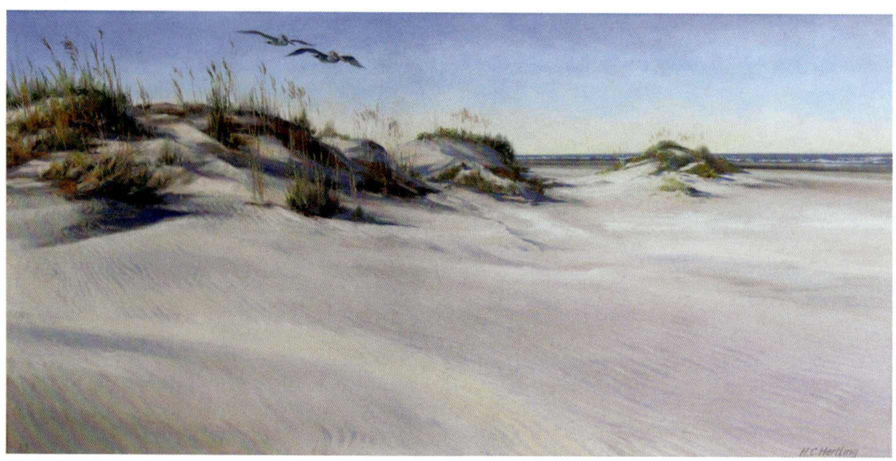

Hangliders, 18 x 36 Oil

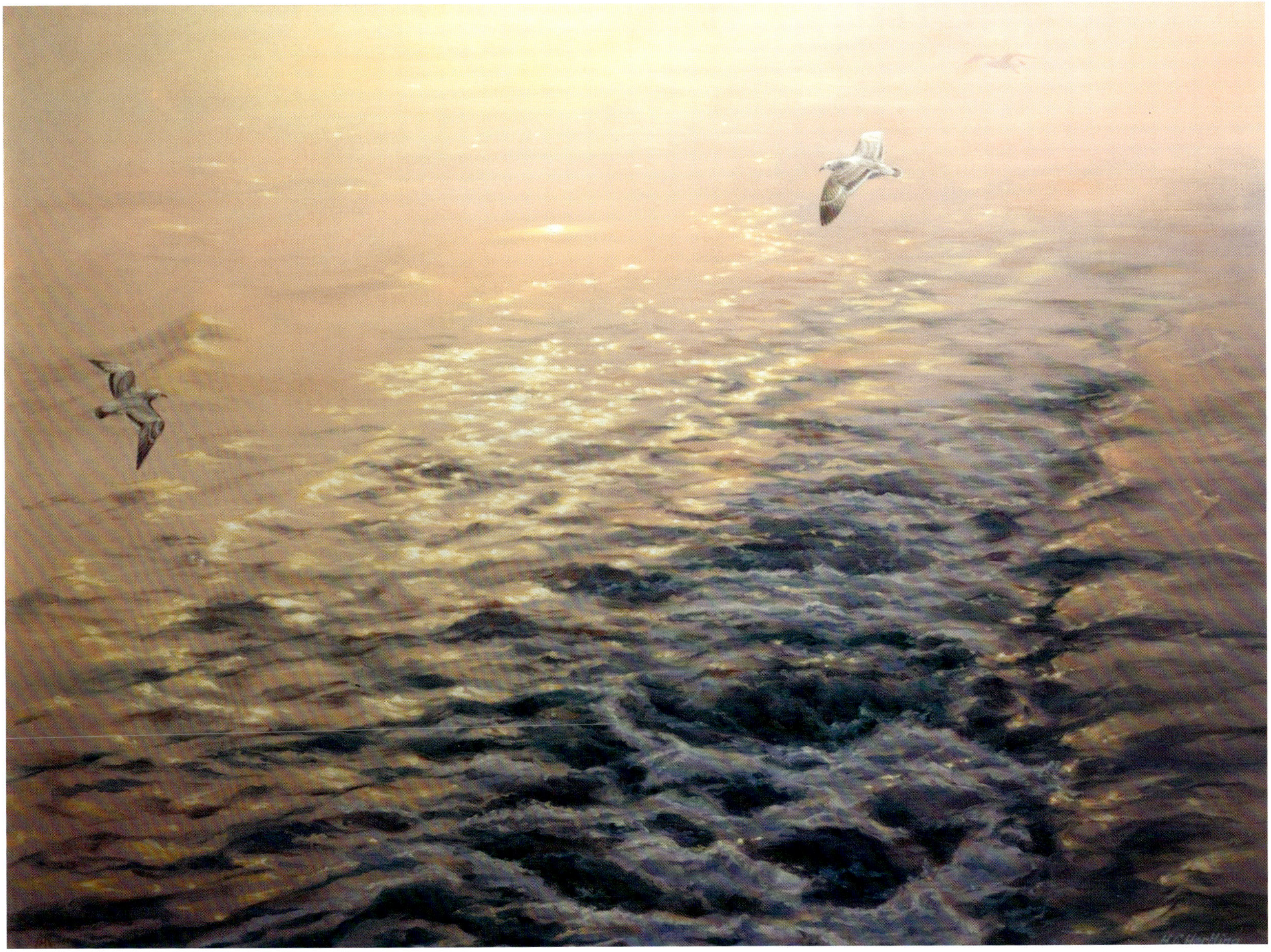

Behind the Ferry, 30 x 40 Oil

When fog dulled the sunset behind the "Badger", the ferry crossing Lake Michigan, the magical light fascinated all of us.

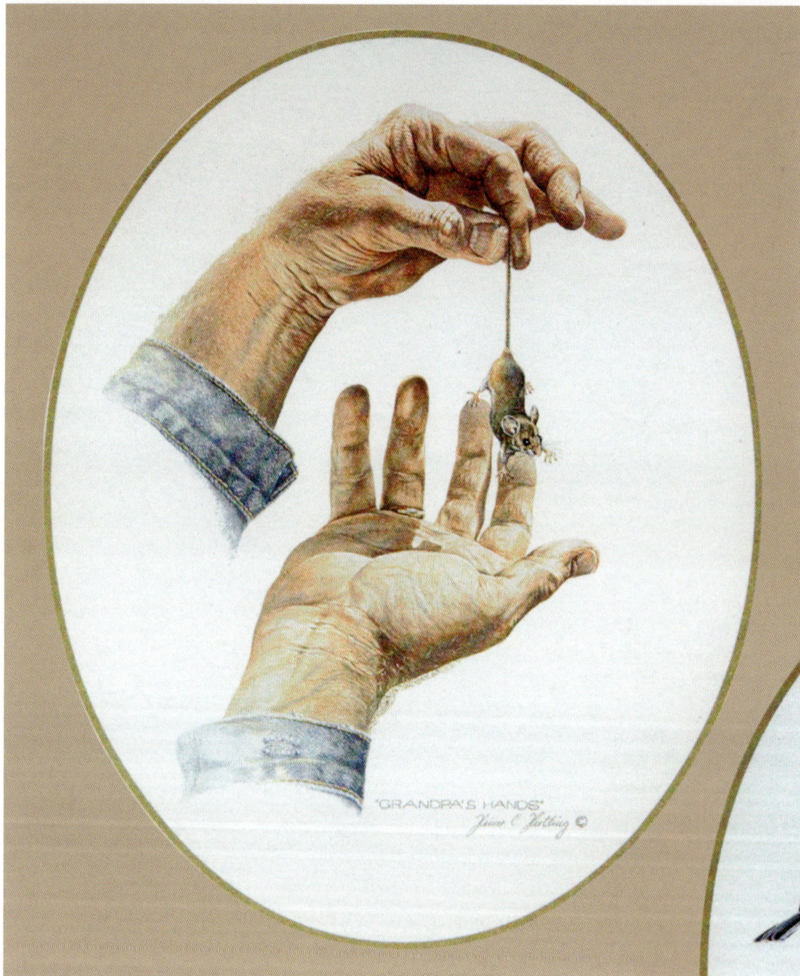

Grandpa's Hands, 12 x 16

Transparent Watercolor on
Illustration Board

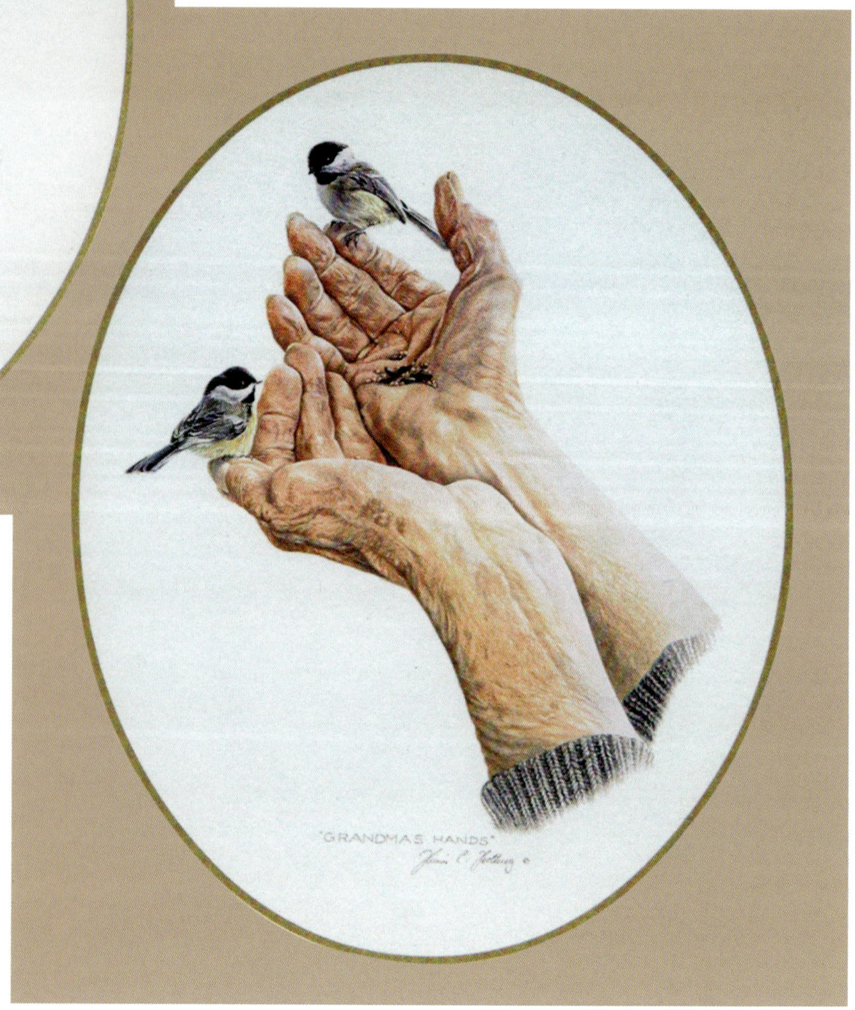

Grandma's Hands, 12 x 16

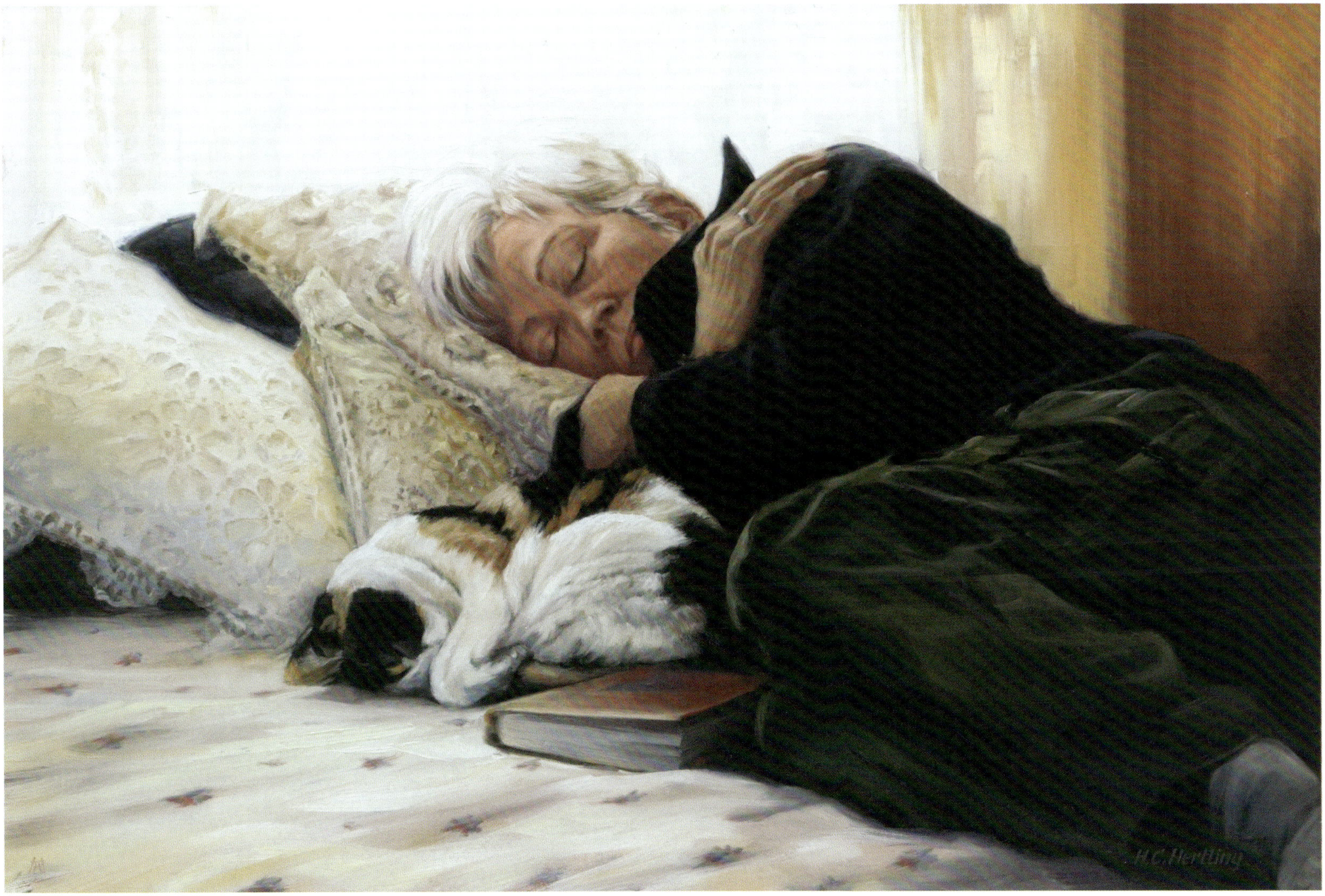

Catnap, 24 x 36 Oil

My wife, the cat Peek-a-boo, and Harry Potter.

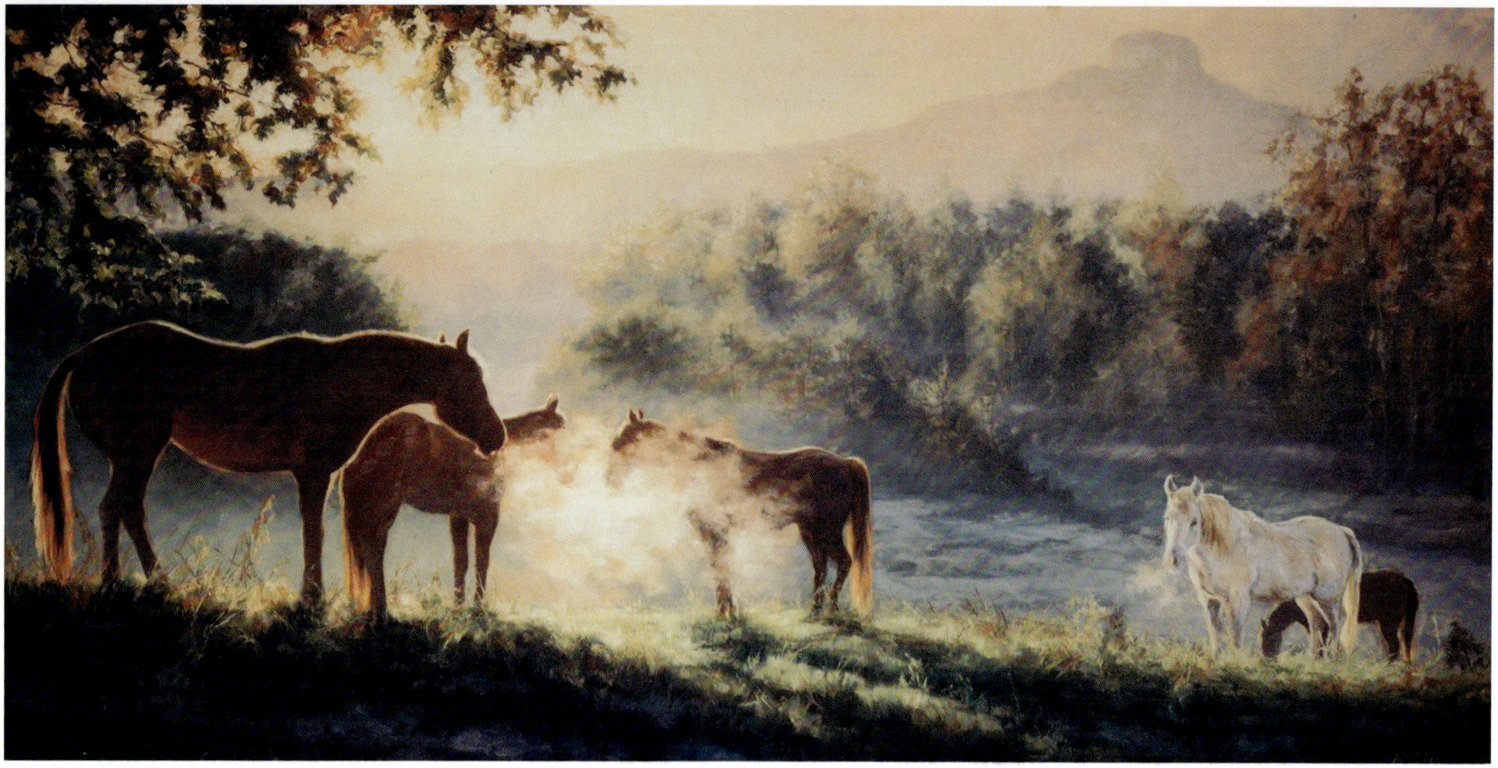

Carolina Morning, 24 x 48 Oil   Pilot Mountain, North Carolina

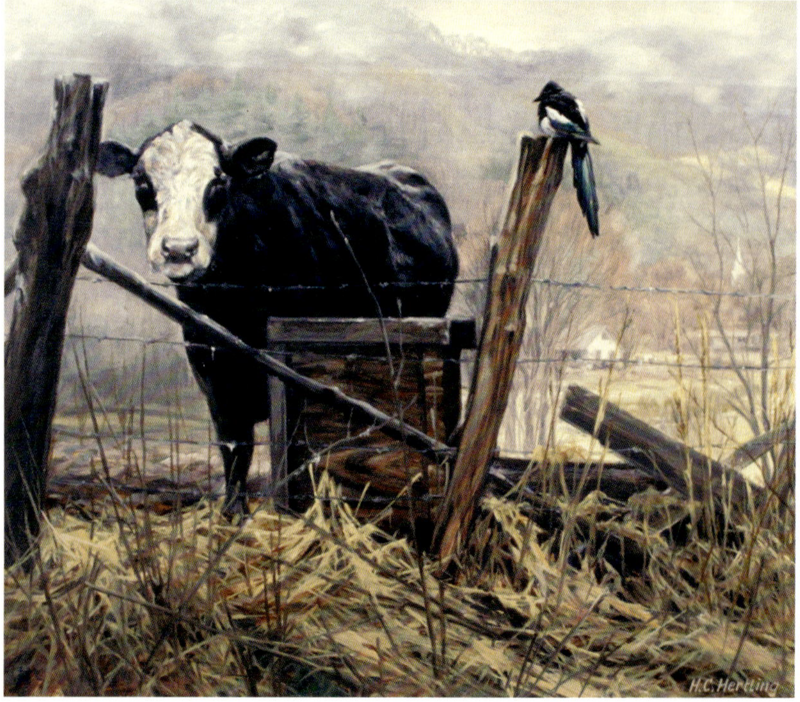

Maggie and Me, 20 x 24 Oil

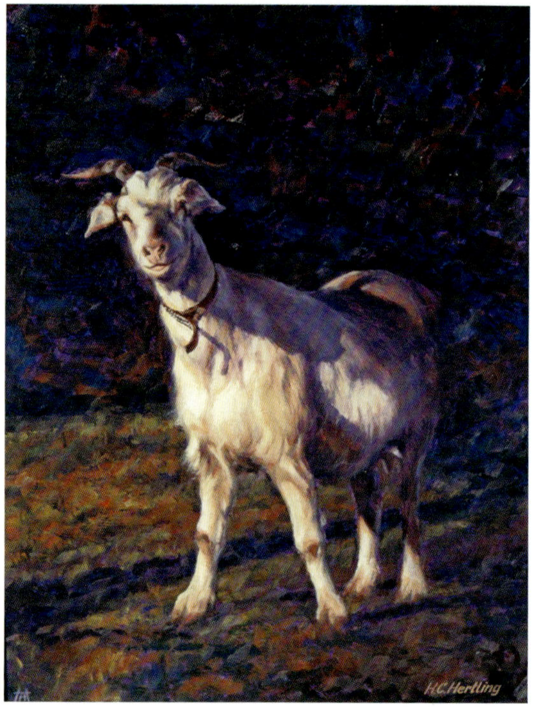

Curious, 16 x 24 Oil

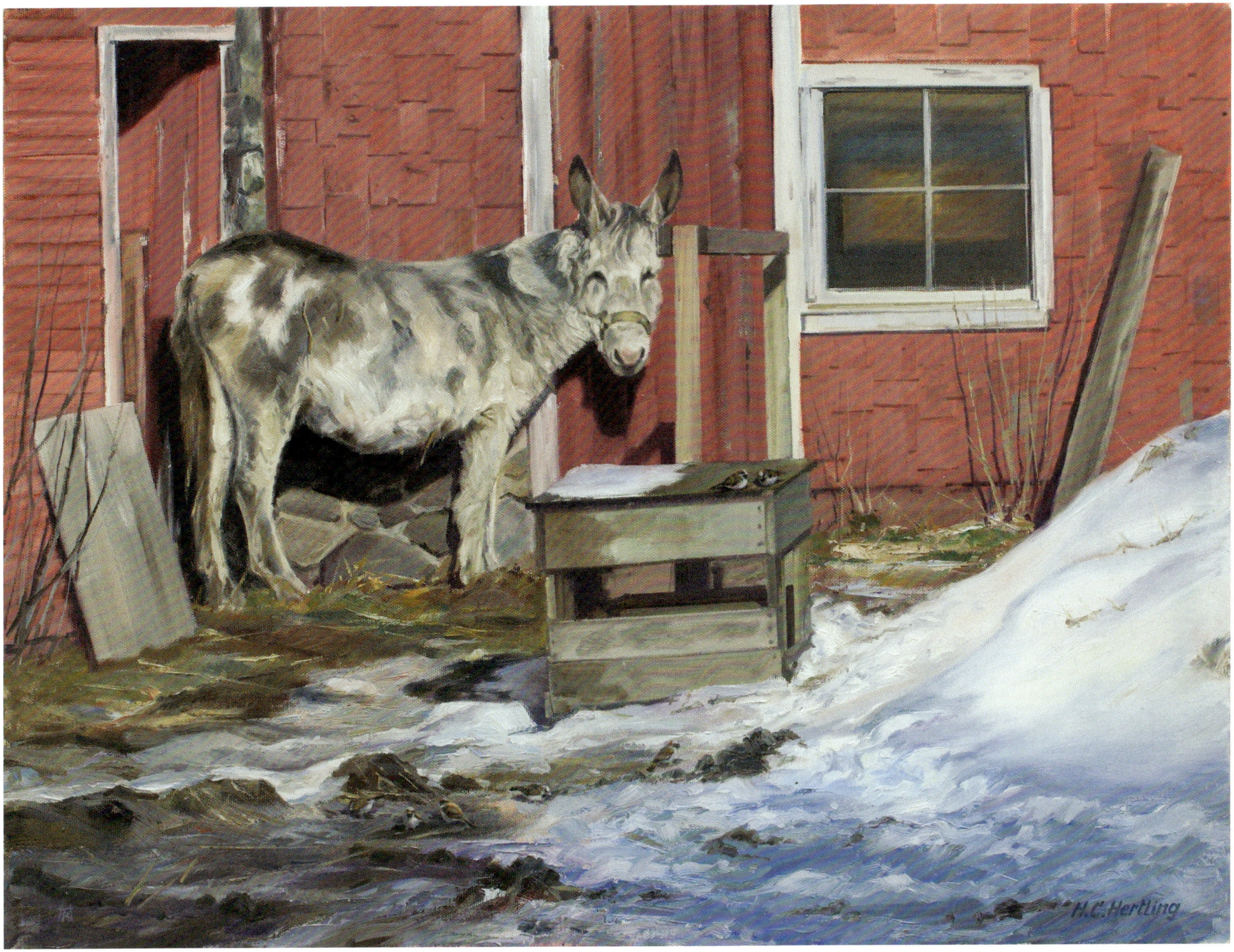

I have an affinity for donkeys and house sparrows. I view them fondly as the animal kingdom's working class.

Plain Jane, 18 x 24 Oil

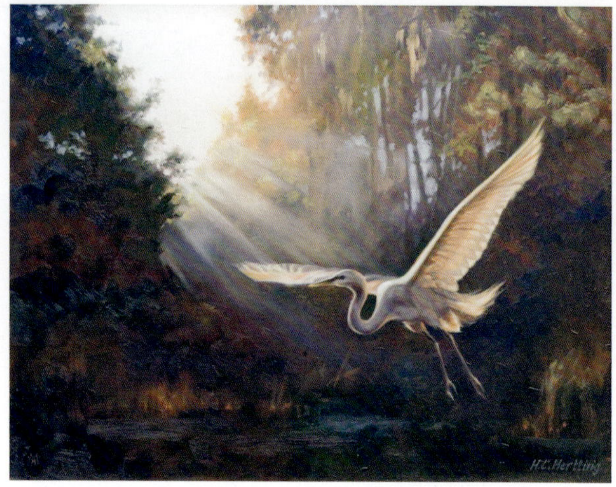

Morning Light, 18 x 24 Oil

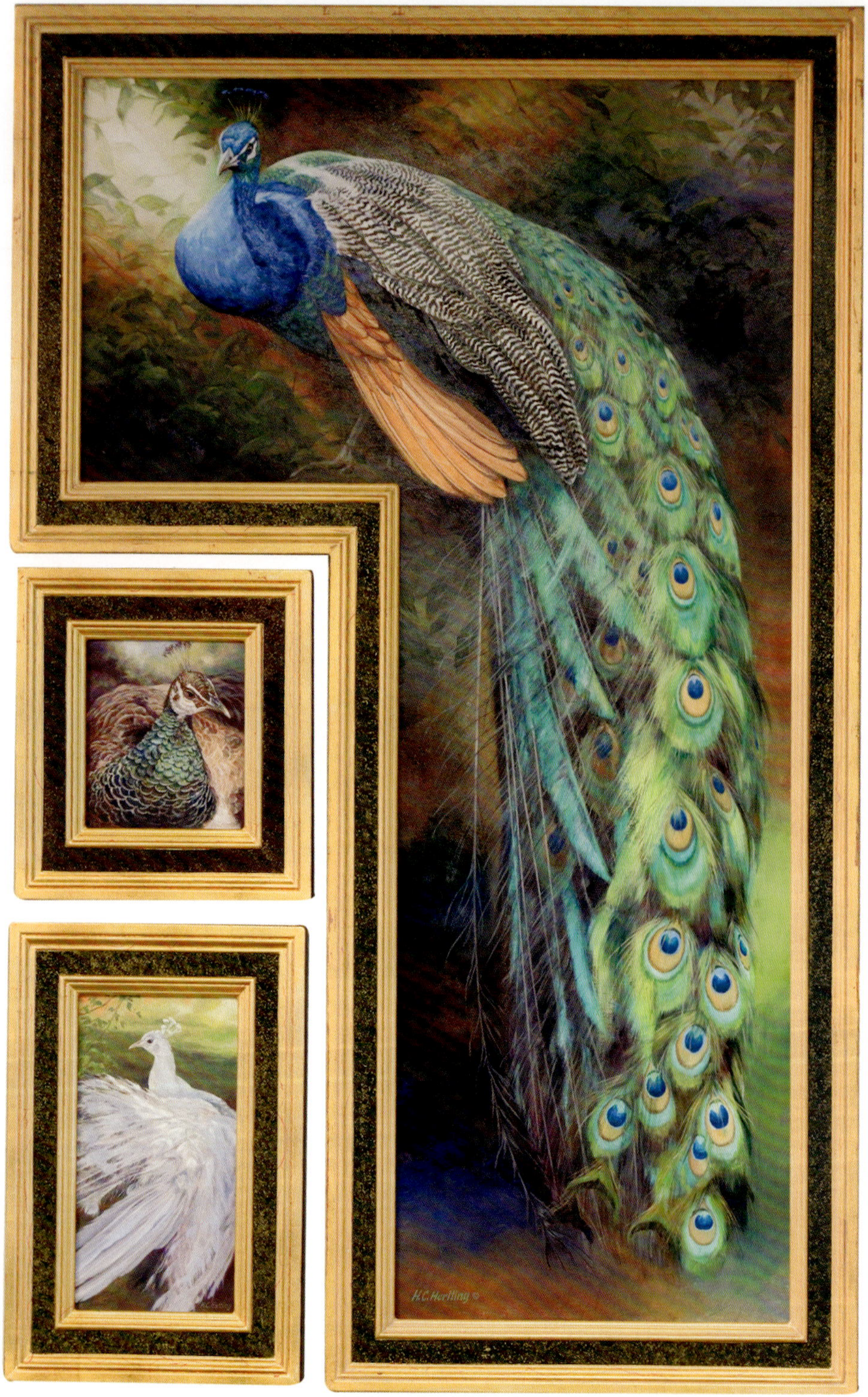

Vanity, 44 x 66 Oil

When creating unusual sizes and shapes as in this triptych, framing becomes a challenge. I like woodworking. I built the frame first and then did the painting.

A thorough three-year apprenticeship in a graphic art studio in my native city Hamburg, Germany prepared me for a successful career in commercial art. My clients wanted to see their products rendered in precise detail. Therefore, I perfected the ability to paint like a camera. That experience took the wonder out of very detailed works of art. But it was a great challenge and a great job.

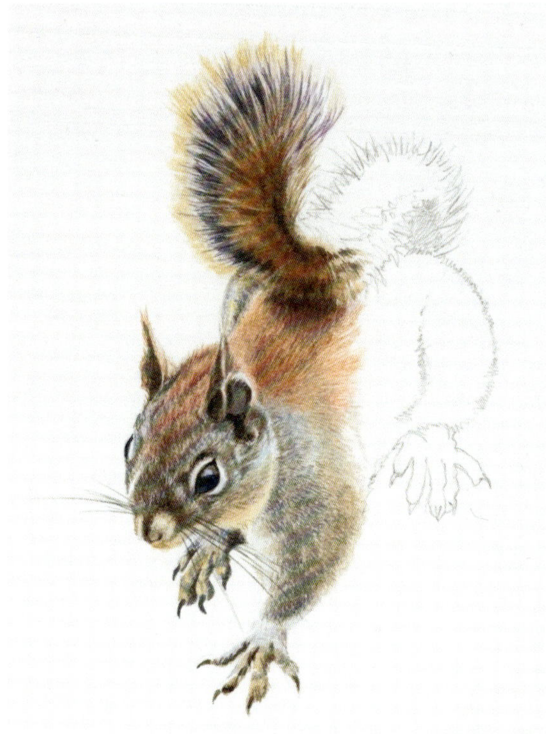

See, he can paint like a camera
but doesn't want to anymore!
Let a camera do it.

Then there is that other thing called "fine art". In my painting I try to involve folks and communicate with them. I want to make them feel what I felt. A good painting lets the viewer discover or sense new things in that piece of art over and over again. I try to avoid spelling things out so thoroughly that there is hardly anything left to the imagination. Perhaps the reason the impressionistic paintings of Singer Sargent and later Richard Schmid fascinate me so much is because I did the tight work for so long. The French Impressionists were also my motivation to strive for a more direct and looser painting style.

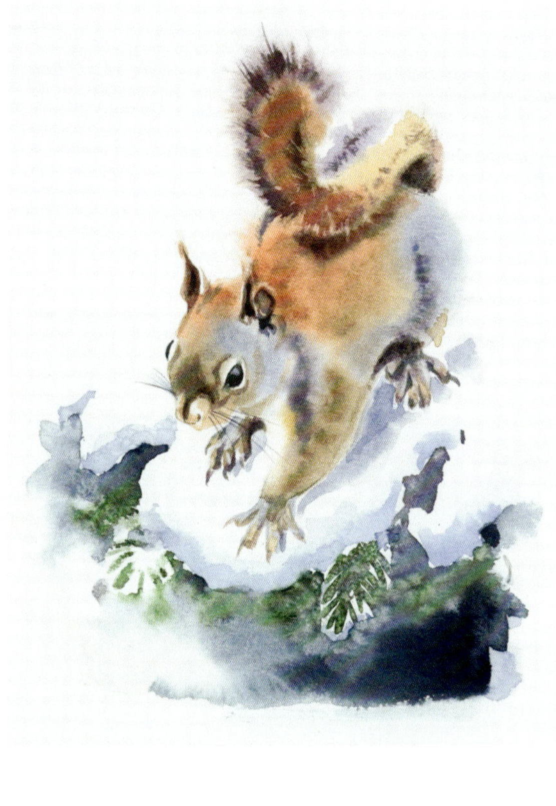

A good poem evokes different feelings in different people. A painting should do the same. That was the challenge I sought when computers hastened my exit from the commercial art studio. It was something new to dive into, studying, reading, asking — anything to get closer to that goal. It is a blessing to know that the goal of perfection will never be reached. I will always feel that the next painting will be better than the last. Welcome to this great insight.

Come on, get off it and help me dig for nuts because the next one will be bigger than the last.

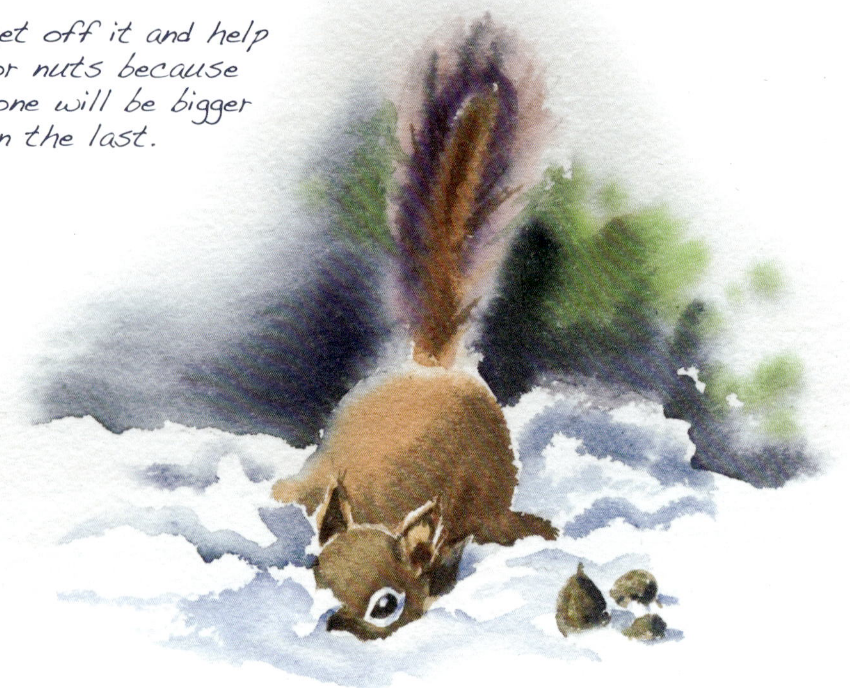

Commercial art training certainly helped me tremendously in my fine art. Knowing what colors do when mixed is just second nature to me. I can't stress enough the importance of practice. Here is a little hint: Before cleaning your palette after a painting session, spend 15 minutes playing. Mix different colors, add white and make mental or actual notes on what you got and how you got it. For example, viridian mixed with alizarin crimson and white can make the most delightful pearly grey. Much better than black and white.

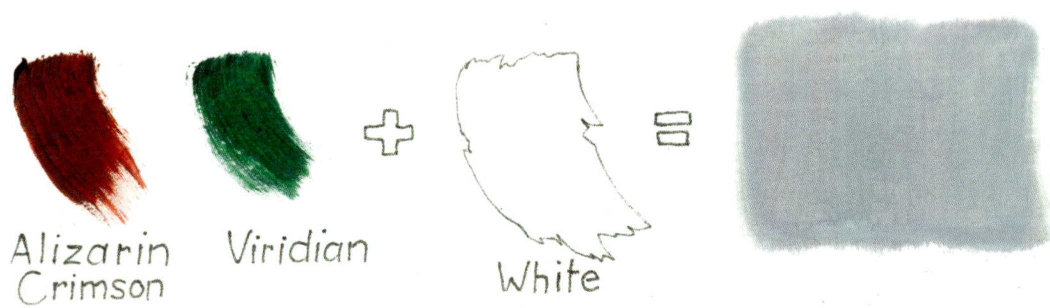

COLORS

Color — the same subject in different light.

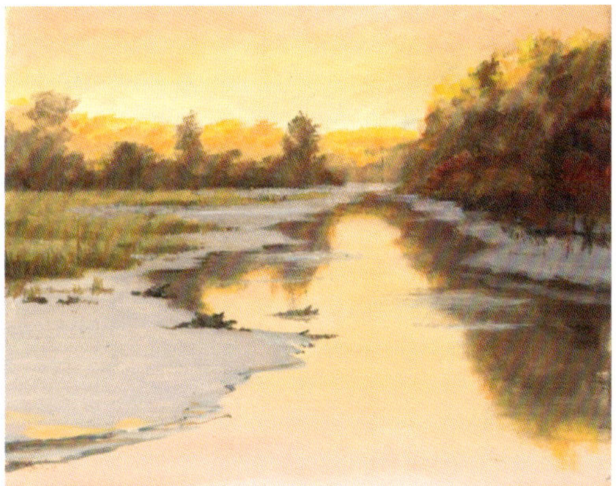
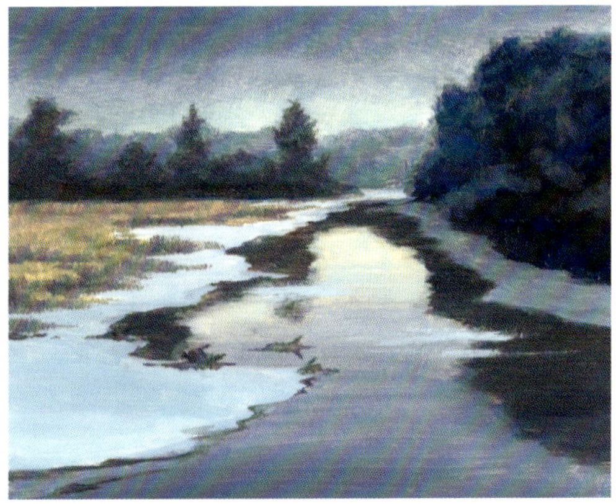

You should know the terms "warm" and "cool" colors. As a youngster I always associated warm colors with fire (red, orange, yellow) and cool colors with ice (turquoise, blue, green).

That sounds a little too simple to me!
I heard there was a cool red (besides me)!

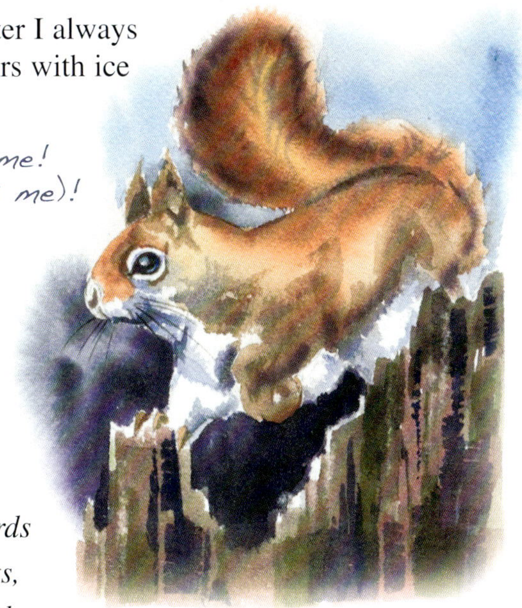

There is a cool red. That just means there is more blue mixed in it compared to a warm red with more yellow in it. For example, burgundy versus orange-red. The same with blue. A cool blue goes toward green, a warm blue goes toward violet. That whole thing is called color temperature.

Painting in North Carolina with a friend, we set up alongside a riverbank. A sudden gust of wind blew my roll of paper towels towards the edge and I ran to retrieve it. Faced with a tangle of exposed roots, I decided to jump over it rather than break a leg, but I ended up on the beach with too much momentum. Splashing head first in the cold April river, I came up minus my glasses and having to retrieve my hat, which was floating downriver. Up on the bank my friend's camera was clicking. The image was published.
You need friends, you know!

VALUES

The value of a color means how dark or how bright it appears. To make this easier to understand, picture a black and white photo or look through red cellophane (available in art supply stores.) You see the values. For example, a red roof of a barn might be darker in value than the green trees behind it, or visa versa. It is very important to constantly check values against each other. This constant comparing holds true for all aspects in a painting.

Color — which is the strongest?
Edges — which is the softest?
Objects — which is the biggest?

That idea of comparison is very important. When I teach workshops, I catch students all the time who have not compared things to each other. When I point this out they say, "Oh yes. Why didn't I see that?" But that is good because it means that I am teaching something. Let's do this so you remember.

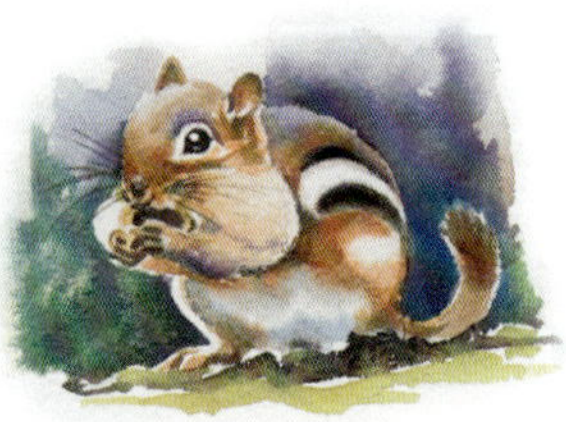

Chippy

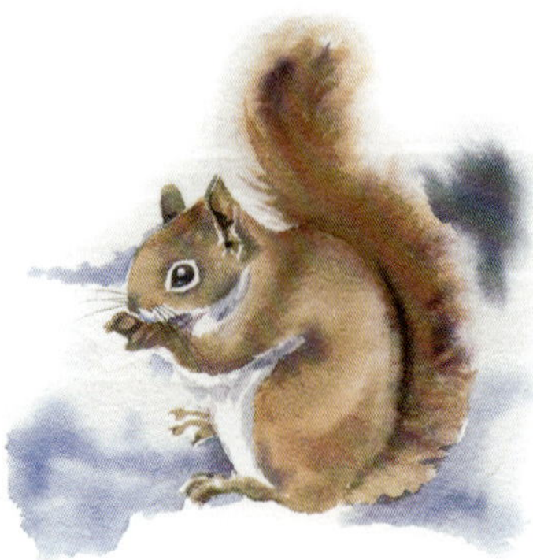

Schneepel

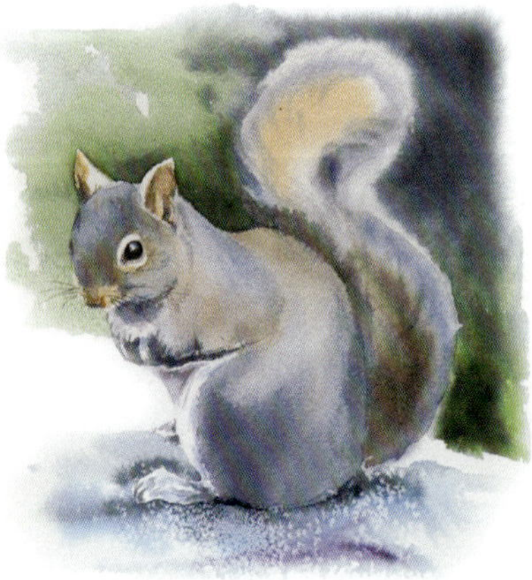

Grey

Schneepel is bigger than Chippy but smaller than Grey. He's brighter in color than Grey but less colorful than Chippy. Sometimes the simplest examples are the best remembered. Thanks for your help Schneepel.

NEGATIVE PAINTING

Once you have blocked in the large shapes, you will want to add more detail. Sometimes this requires negative painting. For example, if the sky is showing through a large tree mass, I use the sky color, but not quite as bright as the open sky, and paint directly over the dark trees. By checking the image in front of me, I start with the biggest holes. Make sure you have soft edges on those little light shapes. Sometimes I run trunks or branches through the sky holes until they look right. Another example of effective negative painting is the dark spaces between lighter grasses. Negative painting can give you very interesting effects.

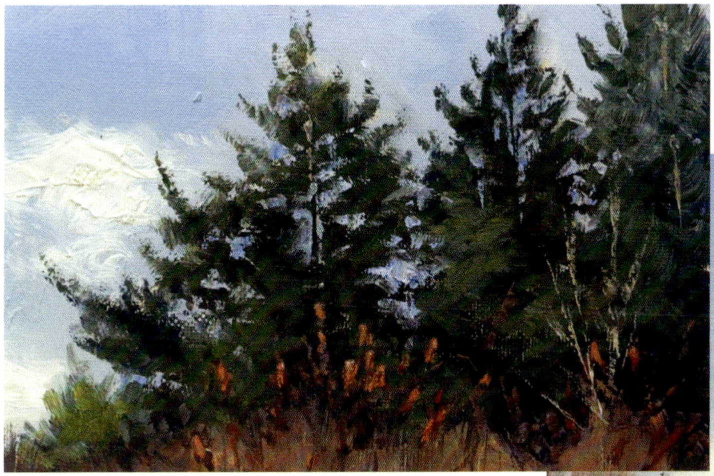

Sky Hole Detail

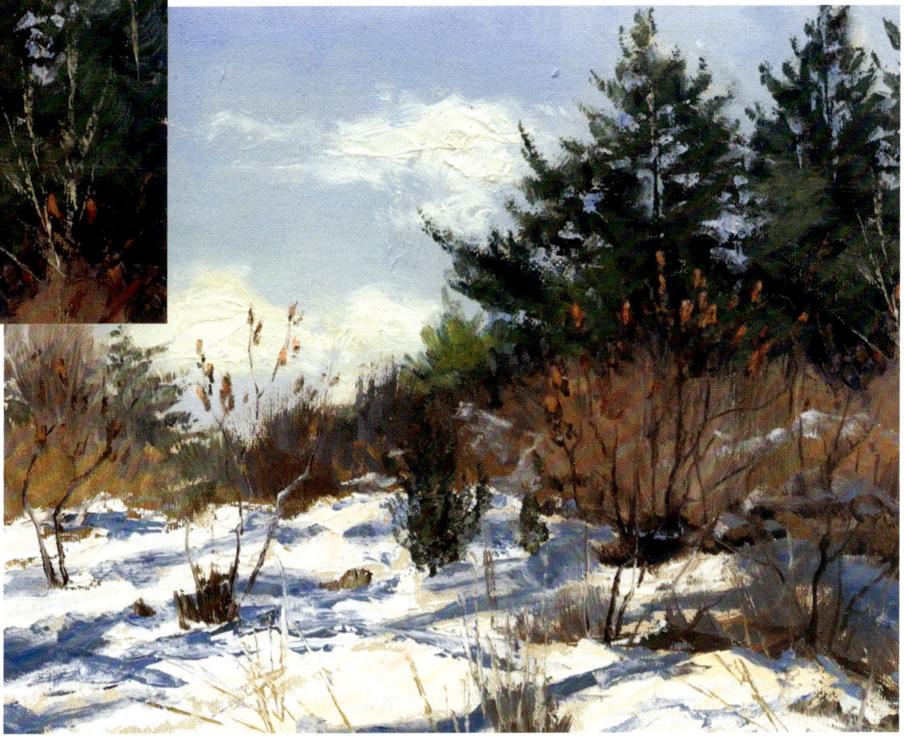

Sumac in Kensington Park, 11 x 14 Oil

STUDIO VS PLEIN AIR PAINTING

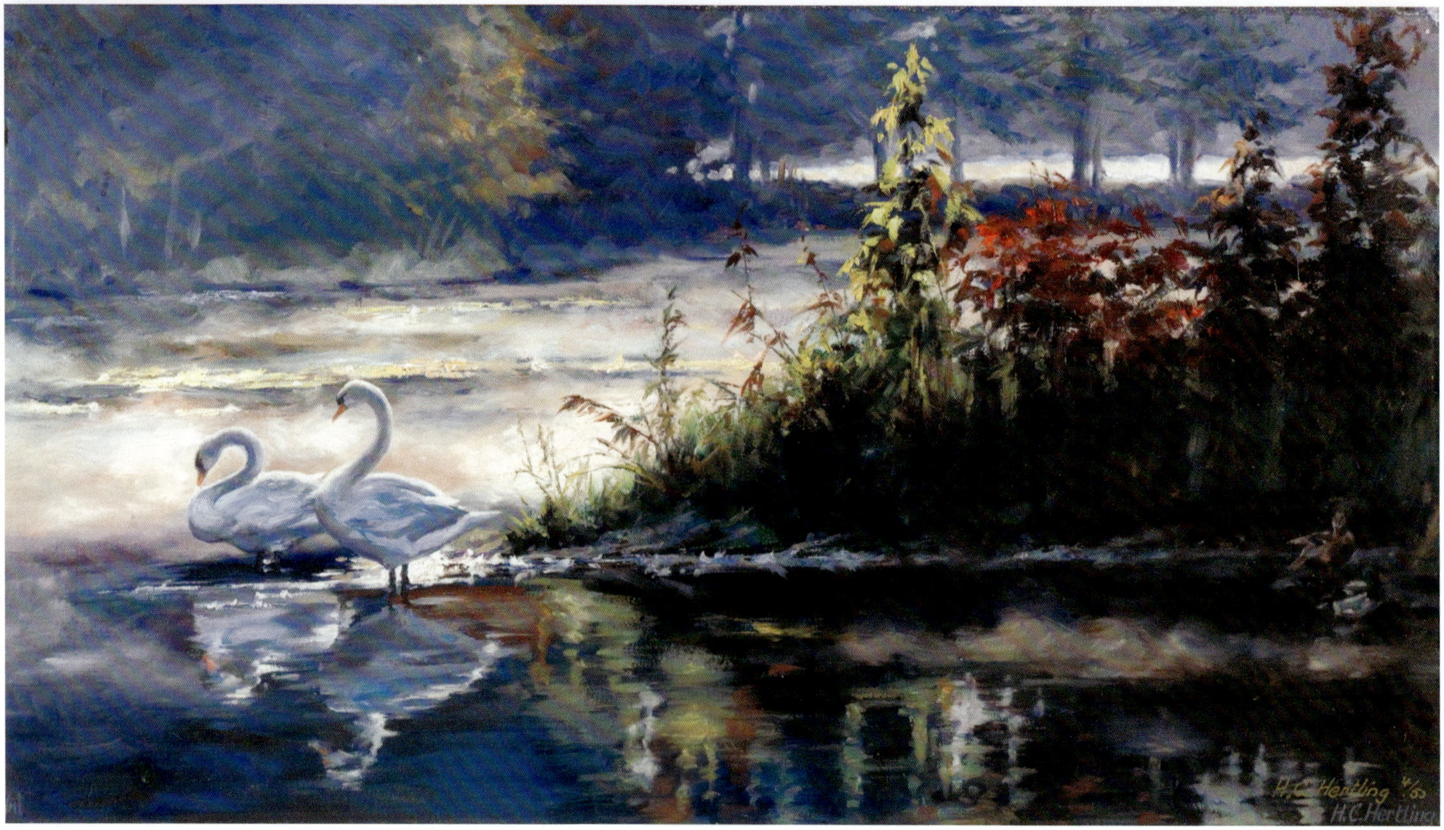

The Landlords, 20 x 36 Oil

Larger, time consuming paintings are best done in the studio. My wildlife paintings often contain backgrounds based on outdoor studies. Mood and color are more effectively captured on location than from a photo used in the studio. Being in the outdoors also gives me clues about what animals to include in my paintings. If you're standing outdoors painting for hours, something will come by — a red-tailed hawk, a fox, a crane or whatever. I often feel compelled to add just that animal. A good example is a painting of swans in our local park. The pair of big white birds was hanging around for a long time. I decided to add them to my painting when I got back to the studio.

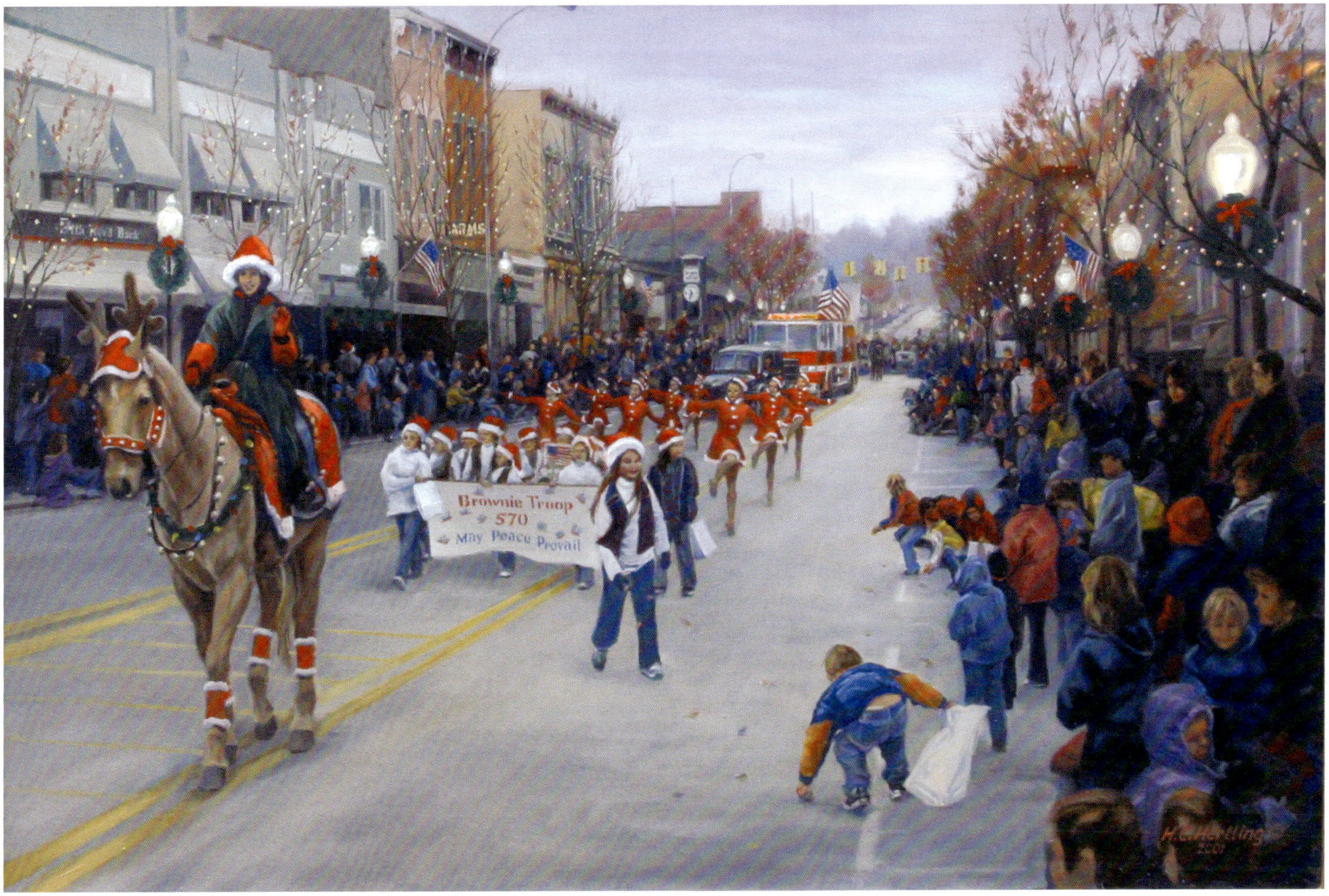

May Peace Prevail, Thanksgiving Parade in Milford, Michigan, 24 x 36 Oil

While painting a street scene during the yearly art show, a young boy watched me intently for a long time. Then came, "Hey, painterman, can I be in the painting?" I agreed and told him to go out on the street where people were walking through the displays. He did and started to walk in place. I told him I wasn't doing a motion picture but he kept it up until I said I was done. He looked at the painting, saw himself, yelped in delight and ran off to get Grandma.

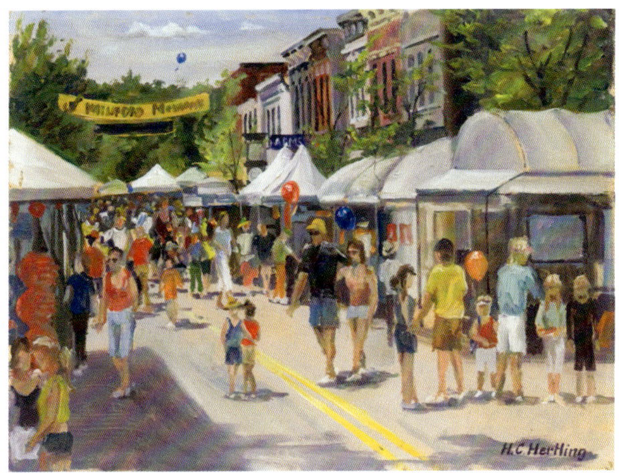

Art Fair Downtown Milford, Plein Air 9 x 12 Oil

EDGES & MORE

Edges are often the most overlooked part of teaching. The correct edge can add or subtract from a subject. A soft (blurred) edge lets the eye glide across the image, a hard edge stops it cold. If a hard edge appears way in the background, it can bring an object forward. Images in the foreground are normally sharper but a soft edge can indicate movement, swaying grasses and leaves. When color or values in your subject are very close to the background color you can have a "lost edge". Let it happen — the viewer will connect the edges in their mind. Make sure you really pay special attention to edges — lost or otherwise — in your paintings.

Enough about edges, here is a good tip!

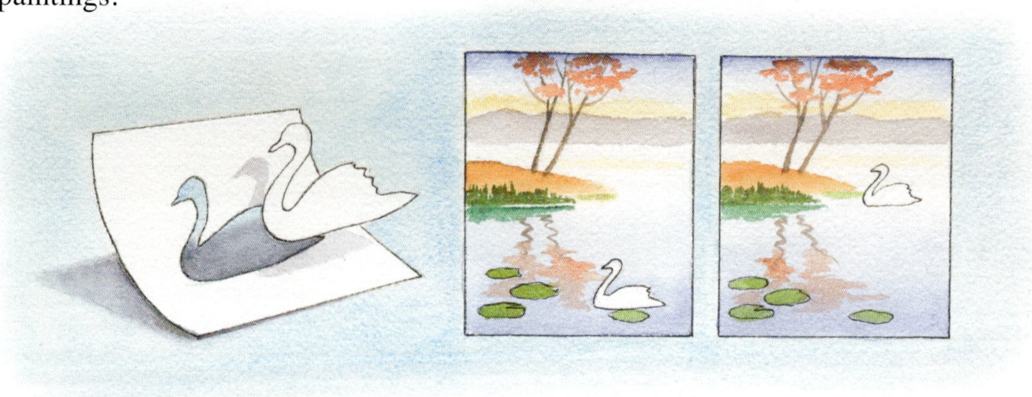

Let's say you decide to add an animal to your painting. For this example I'll use a swan. Draw the swan on a piece of white paper with a pencil. Be sure you have good reference as animals have to be correctly drawn. Cut it out with an Exacto knife and save both the cut-out and the cut-out background. Now hold the little swan on the painting and see where you like the placement. Believe it or not, there is only one right spot where it appears to be the right size. If it is too close up front, you have a miniature white duck. If too far back, you create a giant, eight-foot swan. Once you find the right distance for the swan in your painting, you can go left or right at your discretion. Since you saved that cut-out background, use it as a template. Hold it where you had the swan. With a little white paint and a soft brush, stroke off the paper edges into the hole and presto, you have an outline of the bird.

Now that brings me to KNOWING YOUR SUBJECT.

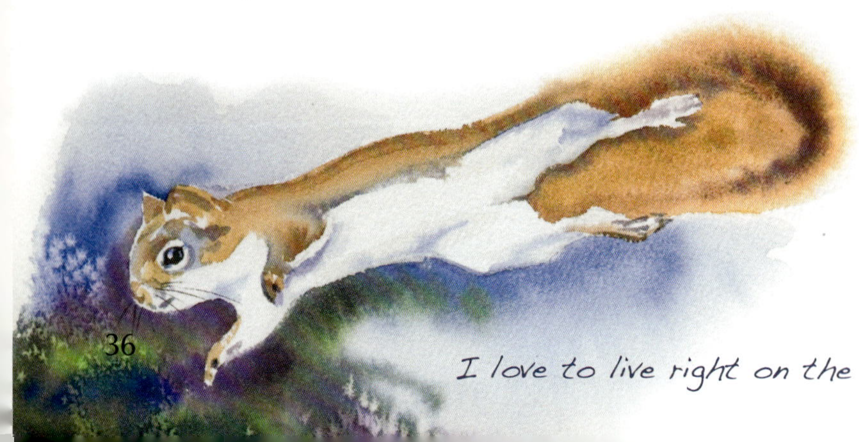

I love to live right on the edge.

REFERENCE

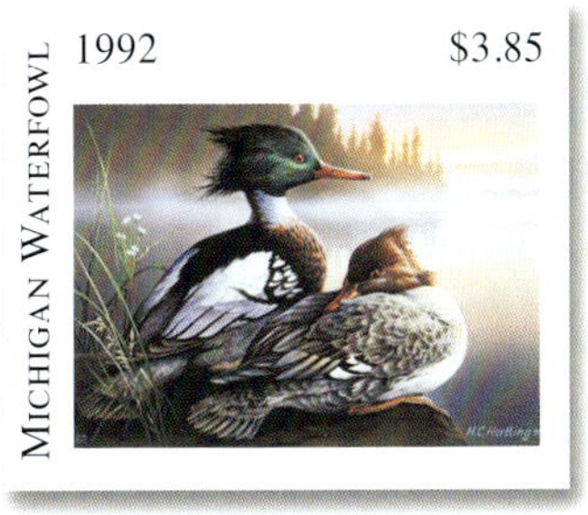

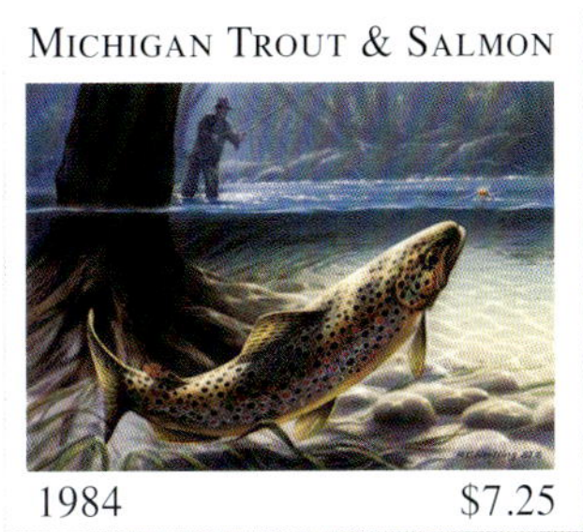

Years ago I got into competing for duck and trout stamps. Those are the stamps a duck hunter or fisherman needs to buy for their hunting and fishing licenses (pretty clever, DNR). Anyhow, I won a fair share of them and learned a very important lesson. Really, really, really know your subject. The first competition I entered was for the Michigan Duck Stamp. A bird carver friend told me about a pond where I could take my own photos of live ducks. It was a great opportunity, so I did. I rendered, with great detail, a pair of pintail ducks and entered it in the competition. Third place was the verdict. Upon asking one of judges about my effort, I was told this would have probably won if the duck's wings hadn't been clipped. Oh well. After that I studied and learned more about ducks than I ever needed to know. But all learning is a good thing.

I told you this story because it holds true for every subject you tackle. If you paint a Civil War painting, you need to know everything about the Civil War. If you do people, know human anatomy. If you do wildlife, study and know wildlife. You don't have to be a hunter. That would be like shooting your model. Even good taxidermy mounts lose their most beautiful aspect, the motion.

It is a good idea to photograph or collect your own reference. If you want to paint an Alaskan landscape, it would be ideal to have been to Alaska. You know what I mean. It gives you a different understanding and familiarity with it. I hardly ever paint (even as a commission) something I don't know. On a dog portrait commission, I always ask to take my own pictures and meet the puppy. It's always a little embarrassing when the poor thing died a year earlier. Oh well, then it's back to commercial art. It's a job and I do the best I can.

If you don't have permission, don't copy somebody else's images. Schneepel, that rascal, always steals from everybody and always looks like he's even proud of it. I watched him once pull a tail feather out of a feeding gentle mourning dove and lick the greasy end of it like a popsicle. Stinker!

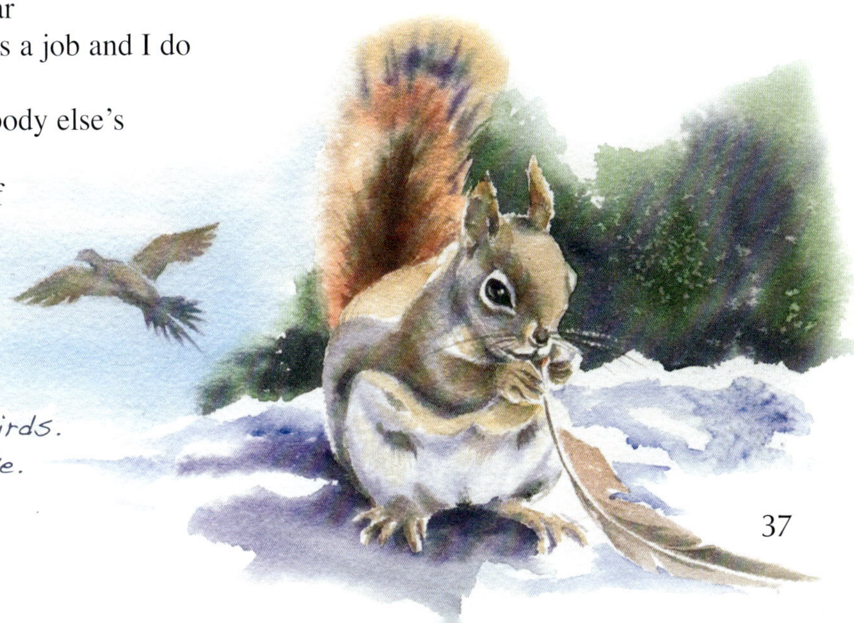

I'm just quicker than those birds. Besides they eat all the seeds I like.

Watch out when painting from a photo. Film or even digital cameras cannot pick up the subtle nuances that our eyes can. The darks in those images are just one color, while your eyes would see the browns, blues, violets and so on. But by having painted enough outside, you remember that in the studio.

When adding animals or birds to your painting, pick a pleasant, characteristic pose of your subject. Just because you have a photo doesn't mean the position is a good choice to paint. The photo could have somebody in it that just sneezed and that isn't the best portrait. I had to throw out a few photos of Schneepel that were not his best side. That's enough about reference.

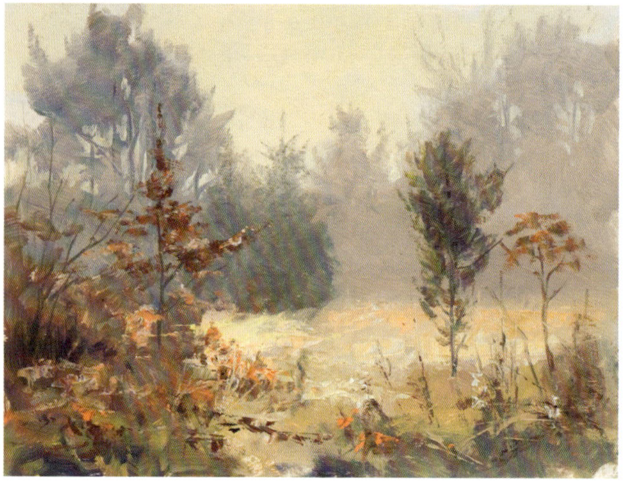

I often get asked how I paint certain moods. Let's pick fog, for instance. Well you wait for a foggy morning and stare at it. Think about it. Were there hard edges? Were there real strong darks and light contrasts? Was there a lot of bright color? No, no and no. If you paint what you just figured out, it might look like fog.

How do you paint water reflections? Again, look at them with more thought than usual. The water, if still, is like a big mirror laying down. Things above it will reflect into it. The blue part is the blue sky. If there isn't a blue sky, water isn't blue (even if your kindergarten teacher told you water is blue). Note: Unlearning is needed. Wavy water is a different story and really needs some studying. Flames in a fire, even though they are constantly moving, will repeat certain characteristic shapes and forms that you have to remember. Waves, again and again let you see for a few seconds repeating patterns that are typical for breaking waves. If you can identify the most often repeated forms, you get a lot closer to creating them on your canvas. Take a picture with high shutter speed and you freeze the motion. But is that what you want? Or is it the constant motion that is so fascinating? Then combine the blur of motion and the shapes you saw. What a challenge!

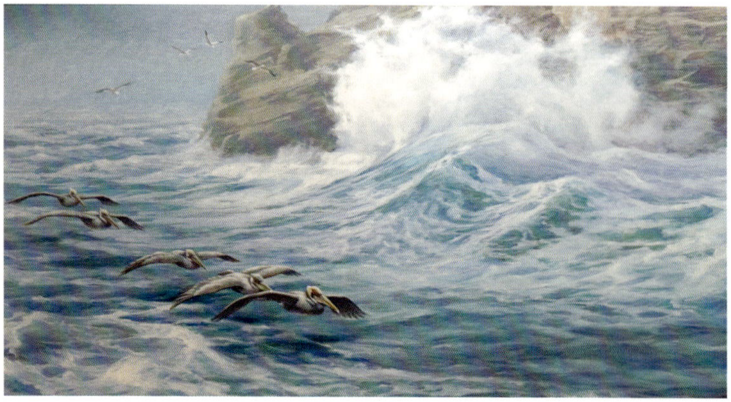

HOW DO I MIX COLOR?

How do you mix a certain color? Well, as I indicated before, try it on your palette or old sheet of paper. A color wheel is helpful. For example, if you want the color kind of bluish, start with blue and add other colors to it. Do a little at a time, you don't want to throw out a half a pound of a color nobody would like.

You see all through our discussions here runs a common thread. Start thinking about the painting tasks at hand a little differently than you had before (if you ever did at all).

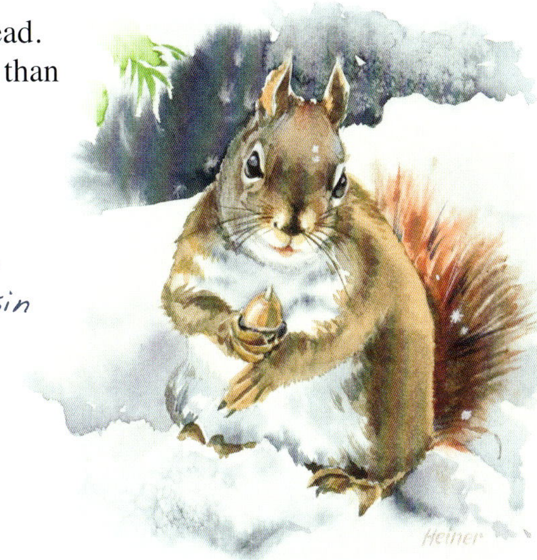

I am trying to change my thinking too! I can't just keeping changing my mind when crossing a street. I just pick a direction and go for it – otherwise I could end up like my cousin down on the road, looking like the flower you tried to press years ago in an old encyclopedia.

WHAT DO I PAINT?

People all respond to different stimuli. Some, like me, are really into the visual. So when I see certain things, even out of the corner of my eye, it sometimes triggers an idea for a painting. Pretty color combinations, a different mood because of lighting, great shapes or something very subtle can spur the imagination. We were painting on a foggy morning and I was taking pictures like crazy when a jogger stopped by and told me to wait until the fog lifts. I didn't get into explaining what I just explained to you because I didn't want to stop him from jogging.

I think that guy stole something. It's the only reason in my mind to run down the road like that.

Commissions certainly take away the question of what to paint. The client has something in mind and you just do the best you can with the orders. But on your own, it should come from the heart. I have learned that my most successful efforts were paintings done just for me. If you start a painting with the idea that it will sell like hotcakes, you probably have a painting that you'll end up owning for years (that's my experience).

PLEIN AIR GALLERY

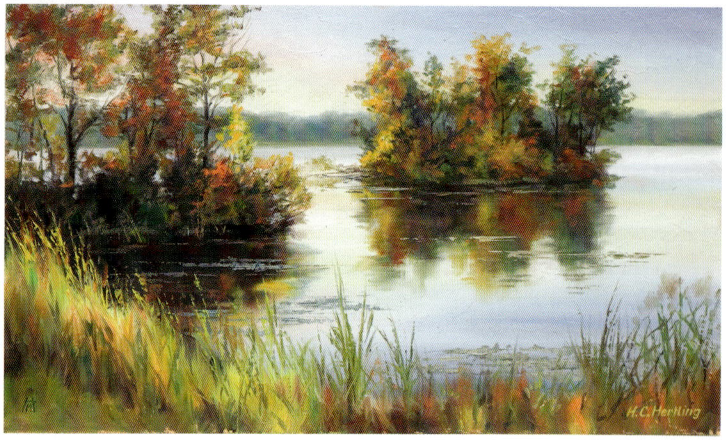

Autumn in Kensington Park, 12 x 20 Oil

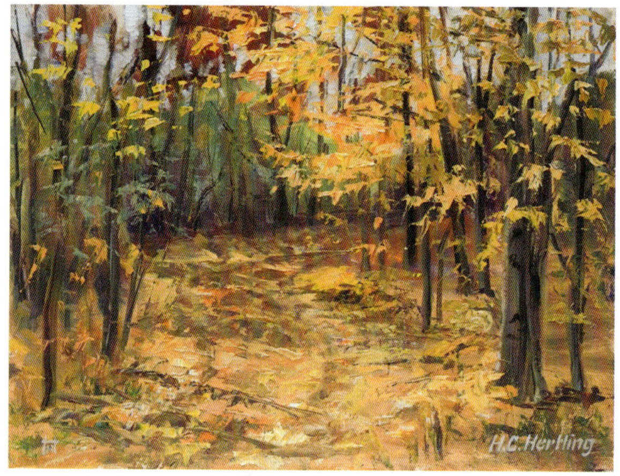

Autumn Woods, 9 x 12 Oil

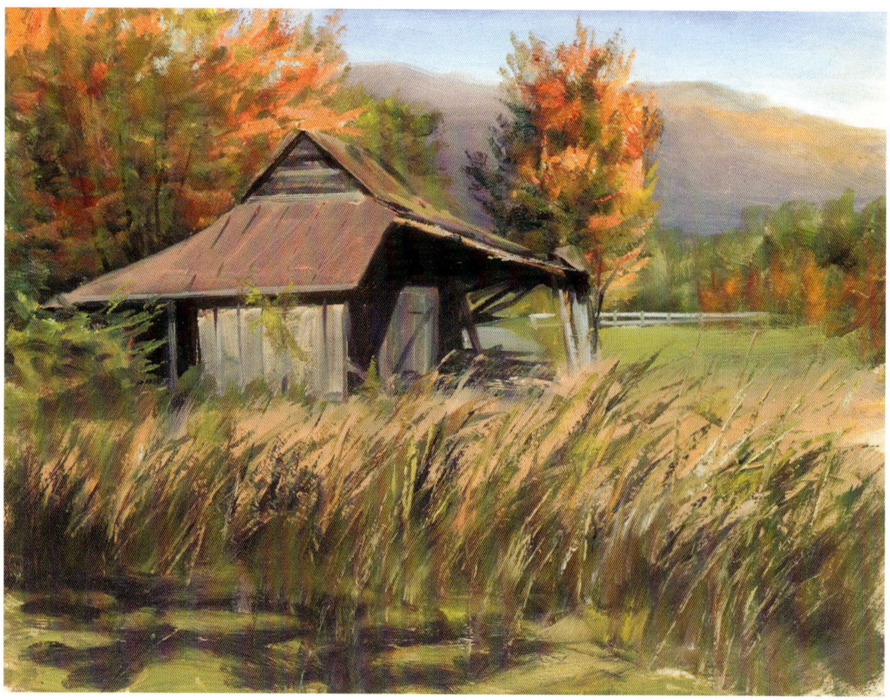

Dave's Tobacco Barn, North Carolina, 9 x 12 Oil

My buddy and I hiked through the deep grasses to a spot we liked and set up to paint. A little while into the session he interrupted my concentration by screaming, jumping up and down and slapping the leg of his jeans. After some weird gyrations, we extracted a big insect, a praying mantis, from inside his pant leg. Yikes! Close call!

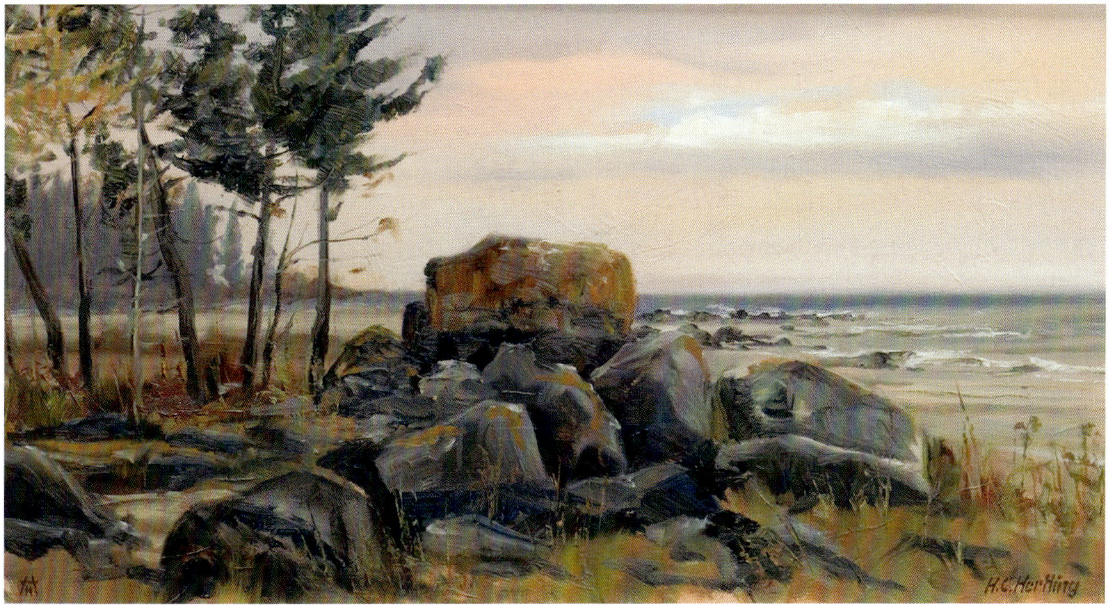
Michigan's Upper Peninsula, 11 x 20 Oil

A young mother with a toddler in her arms was standing behind me while I was painting, telling her son, "See the man is painting the lake and the clouds, the trees and the grass." After a short silence, the response from the youngster was, "Why?" I turned around and for once I was speechless.

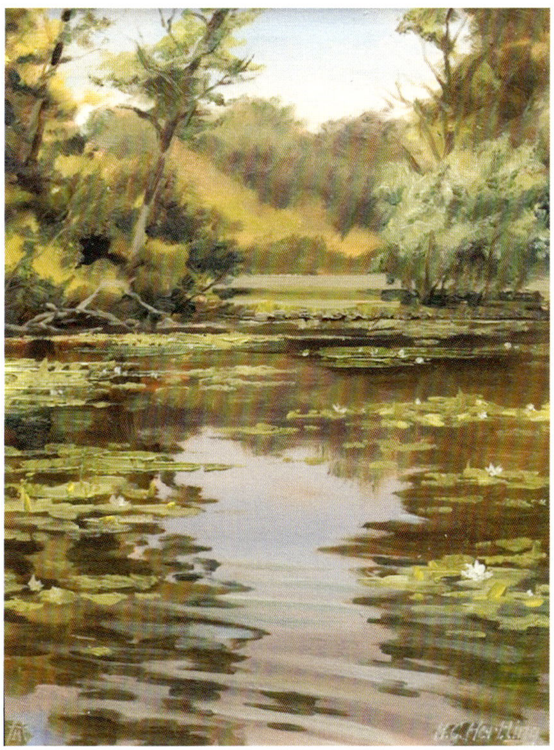
Water Lilies in the Park, 11 x 14 Oil

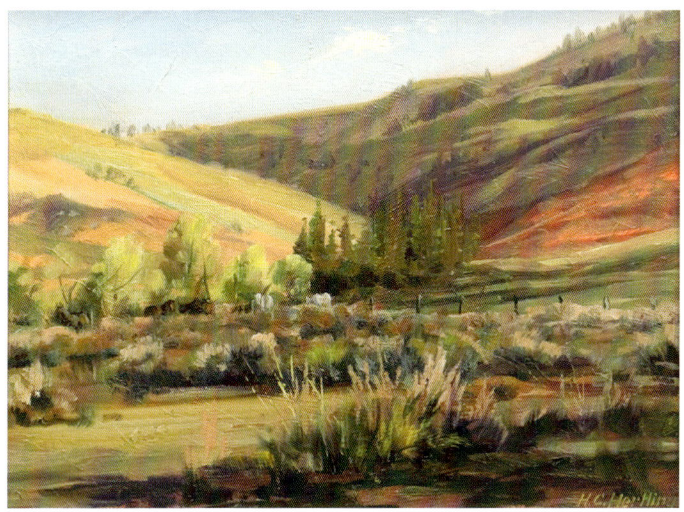
Outside Dubois, Wyoming, 9 x 12 Oil

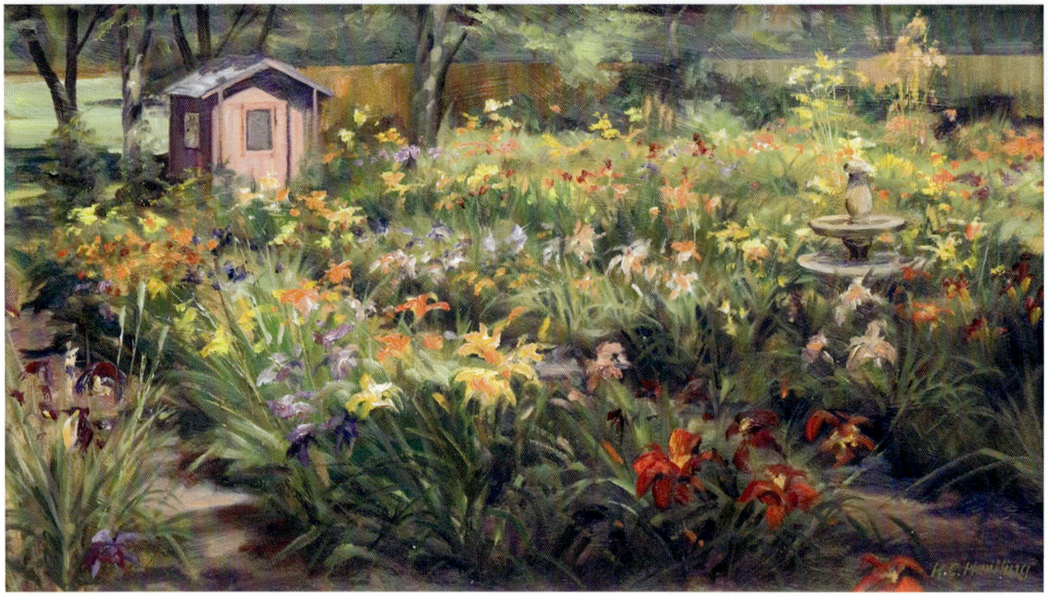

Diane's Daylilies, 11 x 20 Oil

Plein air painting at a local nature center for Earth Day, brought our group "Michigan Plein Air Painters" out in force. Two of my friends set up side-by-side to paint an old barn. They caught the interest of a little boy about 10 years old. He watched for quite awhile. Then he decided to offer his opinion. The first lady heard, "I like your painting." The second painter got this comment, "Yours looks a little rushed." Priceless to the rest of us. That kid will probably end up in politics.

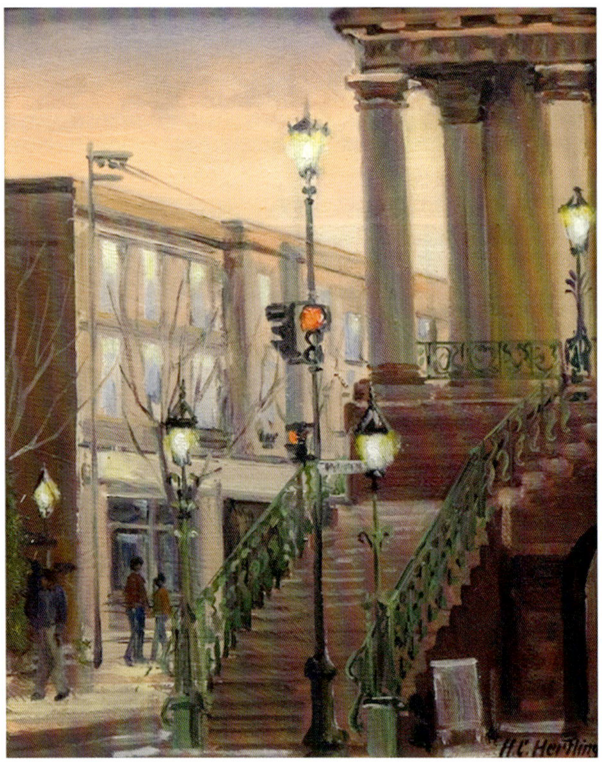

Market Street, Charleston, South Carolina, 9 x 12 Oil

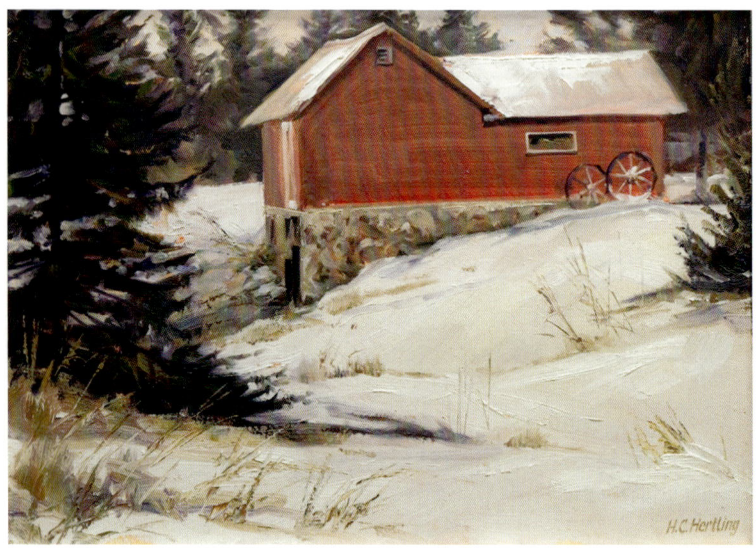

Neighbor's Barn, 11 x 14 Oil

CRITICAL ONCE-OVER

When I bring a plein air painting back to the studio, I do one more important thing. I set the painting up and let my eyes sweep back and forth across the image. If I get stuck on one area or thing that doesn't look right, I alter it, often with my finger. It might be an inappropriate edge, value or badly drawn brush stroke. Don't rework your whole painting. It is after all an outdoor painting or sketch.

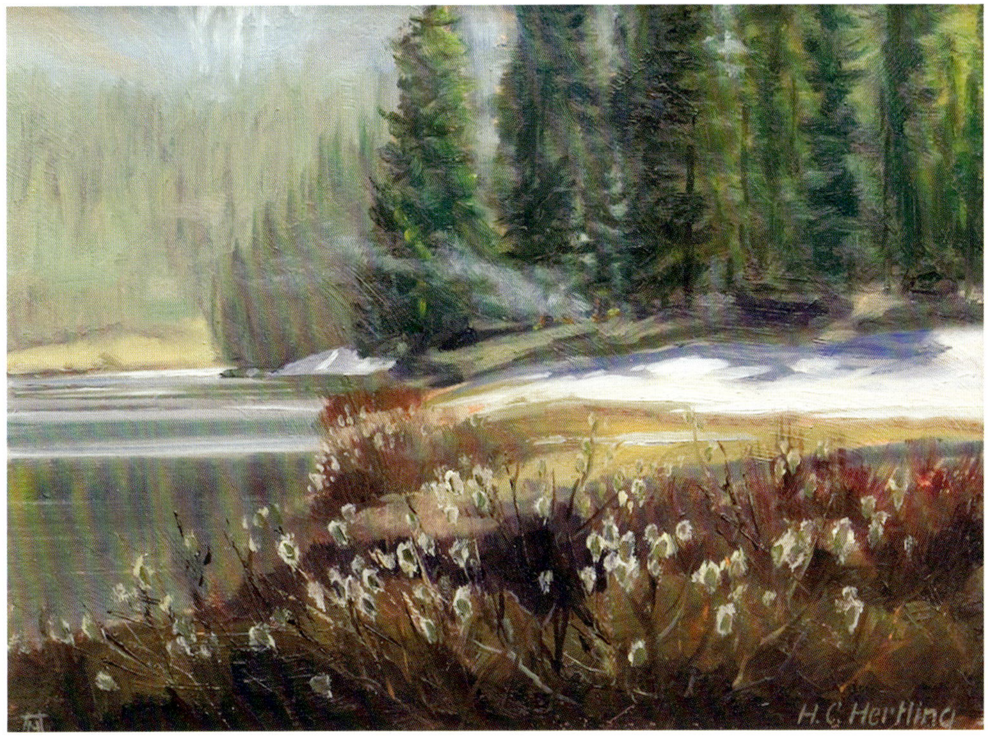

Camping on Brooks Lake, Wyoming, 11 x 14 Oil

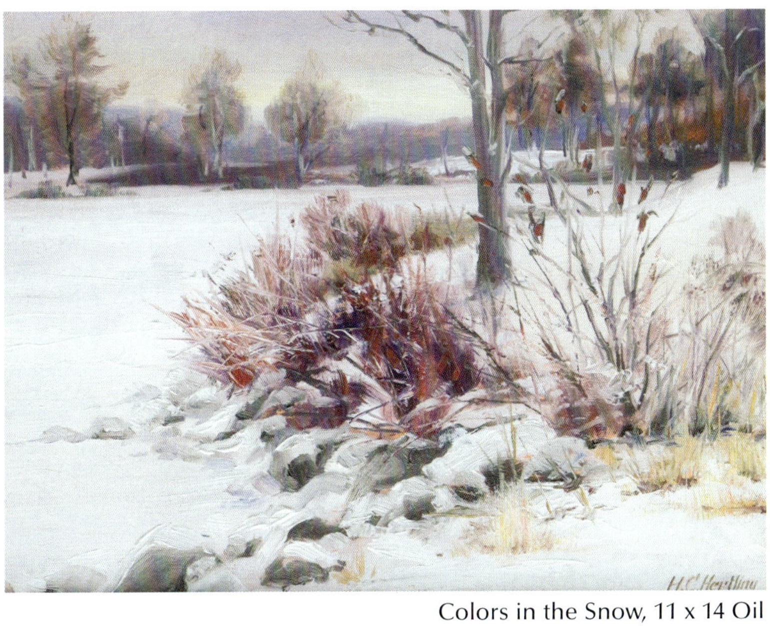

Colors in the Snow, 11 x 14 Oil

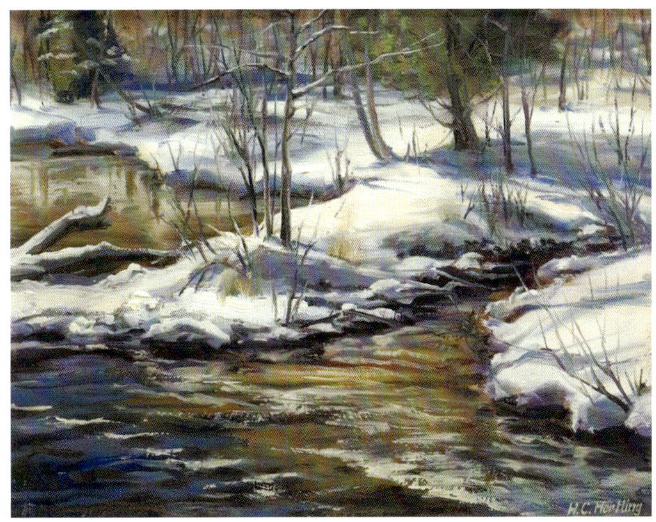

Winter in Kensington Park, 11 x 14 Oil

CROPPING

A cropping tool is a view finder or any cardboard frame that you hold up with an extended arm to choose your scene. Move it around until you see a nice well-composed and balanced image within that frame. It cancels our peripheral vision and picks one area out of a very overwhelming and complex scene. Some of my pet peeves are: things put on the very edge of a canvas (the frame would probably cover them up); horizons that slide down to the side and make you feel like you are falling out of the picture; and crooked water surfaces. Things dead center are not appealing either. If you can't find the perfect or desired crop, it is perfectly fine to move things around (artistic license). Photographers could not do that until PhotoShop came about. I admit to having changed the crop of paintings on hardboard with my table saw.

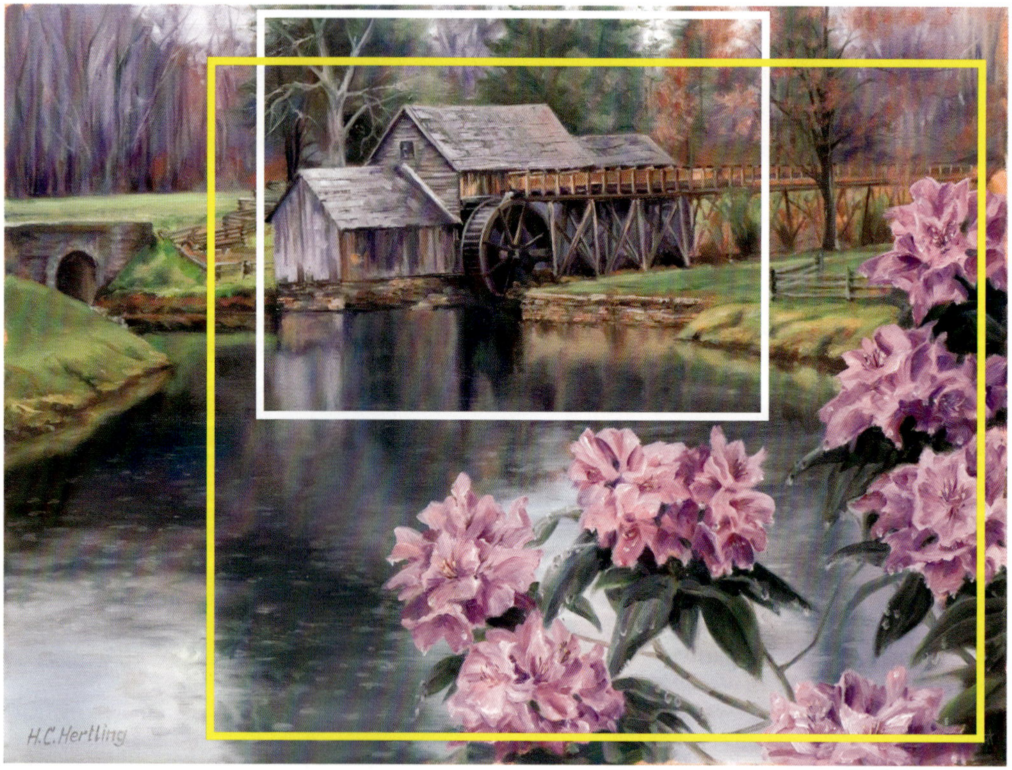

Purple Rain, 18 x 24 Oil

CHANGING YOUR OUTLOOK

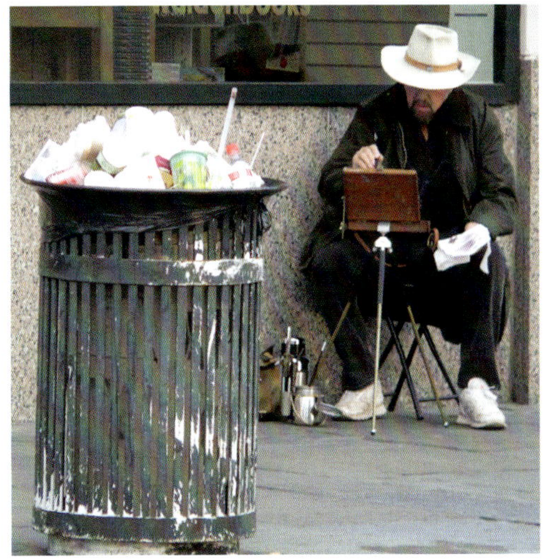

My friend and fellow artist, John Seerey-Lester working in Charleston, SC, seeing something beautiful in everything! Just kidding — he was actually painting the market street past the garbage can.

We've talked a lot about looking at things in a new way. This new outlook can be carried over into other aspects of your life. It is best illustrated by a little story I experienced with my daughter who was born with defective vision. She has handled it just fine and does to this very day. When she was young we lived on a lake. It was morning on a grey, cold and, what we might call, miserable day. I was looking out at the drizzling scene when she came up behind me and said "Look Dad, it's all soft outside." It probably wasn't her intention, but it triggered something in me and I am grateful to her still.

What a wonderful way of looking at the world differently than everyone else does. I looked at the subtle tones, silver hues and harmony on our lake that morning. It occurred to me that squinting is the very tool to get you to see what Wendy saw.

So go painting on a grey day in November, paint an opossum that everybody considers ugly, find a scene behind a machine shop or alley or a fallen shed. Try to see nice shapes, colors and textures. Now you are growing into an artist. Maybe you can look at other situations in life differently, too.

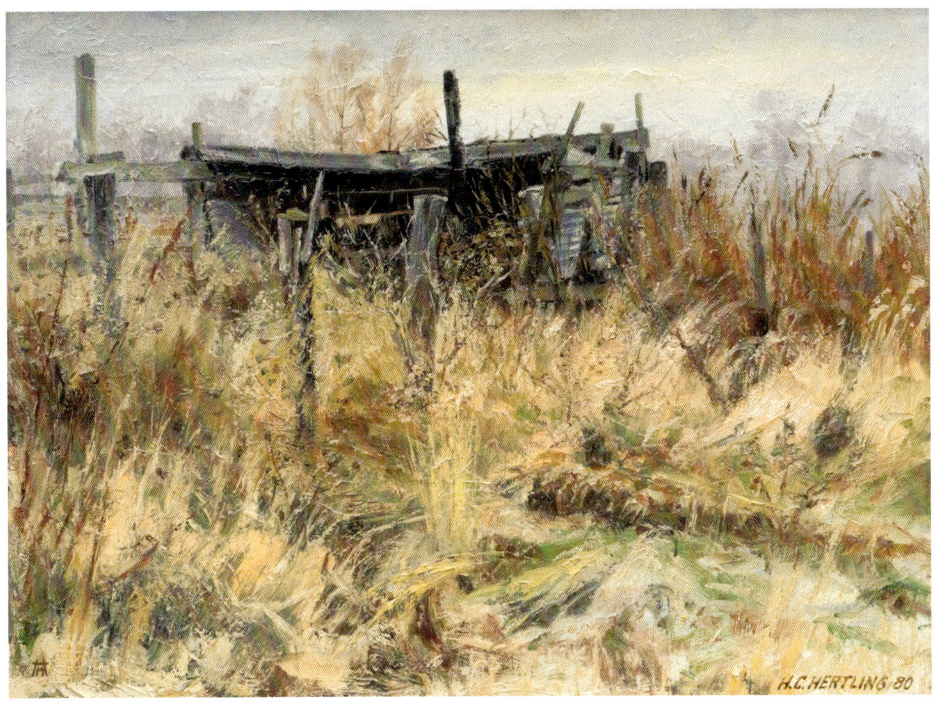

The Old Shed, 11 x 14 Oil

ECONOMY OF BRUSH STROKES

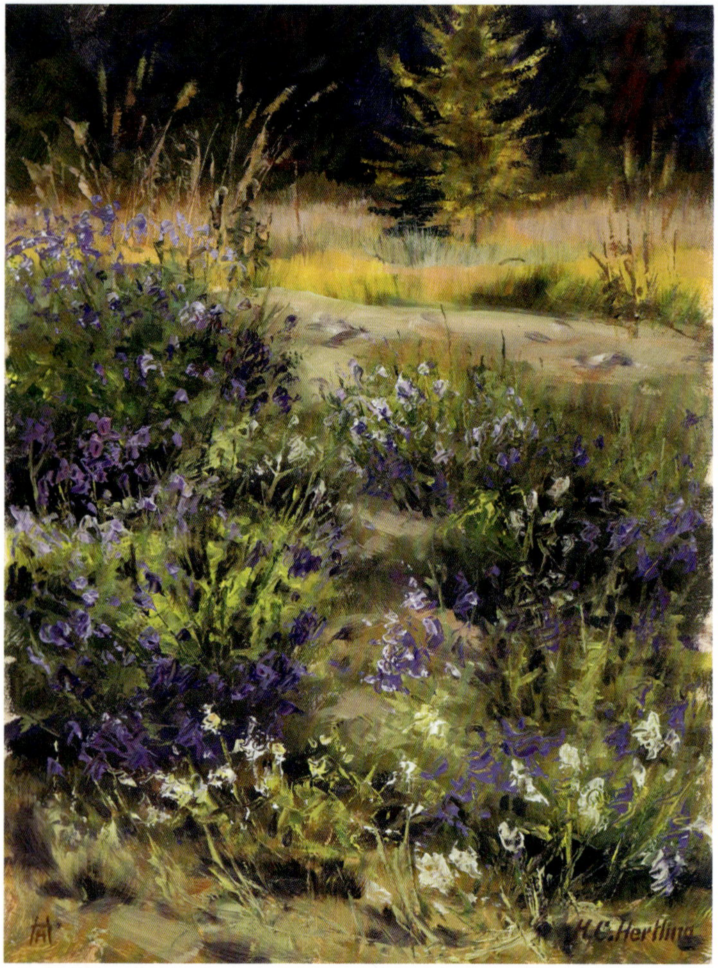

Alfalfa Blooming, 9 x 12 Oil

Now there is a concept. Not only has the economy something to do with sales, but it controls the pure color, the painting time and the fresh appearance of your painting, too. It means eliminating unnecessary brush strokes. Like any mixing process, the longer and more vigorously you mix, the more even the mixture. If there is wet paint on your canvas and you want to add a new, different color, you better limit your stroking. For example, if you want a yellow stroke on a blue background, you better make only one stroke. The next one would mix the blue with the yellow and you would make green. I often hear the complaint, "I am making mud". This is the direct result of too many brush strokes. Once you've got blue, red, green and white on the board and keep stroking around in it, you end up with a color that only works on a military jeep. The color is a dirty green often seen in old paint thinner, on never-cleaned palettes and on old brushes.

Another plus of this economy business is that it gives your painting a fresh, direct and secure appearance. It looks like you knew exactly what you were doing. Every stroke was the correct color and shape. It takes a lot of practice and experience but is certainly worth striving for. Just tell your brain to ask your hand not to let the brush flip around on the painting. Sometimes a student makes so many strokes with the brush so fast that there isn't time to check if one of those strokes was the desired one! Slow down and look every time your brush touches the board. Think about your "economy of brush strokes".

ONE MORE STEP-BY-STEP

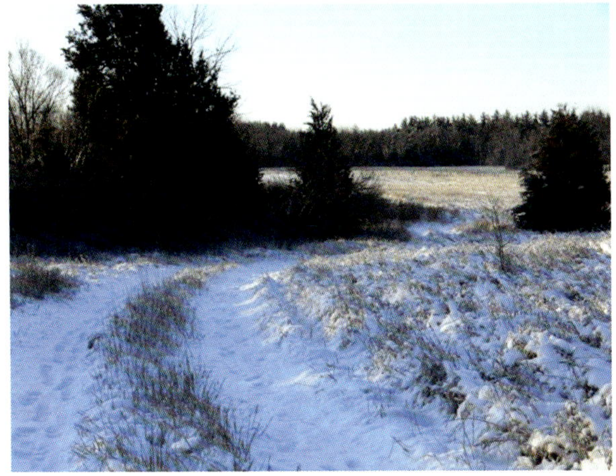

This is a great image to demonstrate the way to create a 3-dimensional looking landscape on our 2-dimensional canvas. There is the simple shape of woods in the distance. There is an interesting, colorful middleground. There is a textured foreground with beautiful leading curves pointing to our focal point, the place where the road disappears. The blue shadows on the snow, the golden grasses, the powerful dark evergreens and the grayish pink of the Red Osier Dogwood make this a colorful winter scene. Let's try to paint it with direct, simple brushstrokes and not get stuck on some detail in the scene. Always keep the whole image in mind.

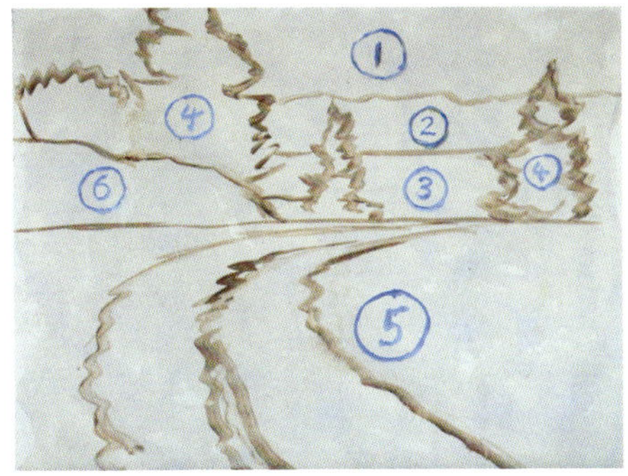

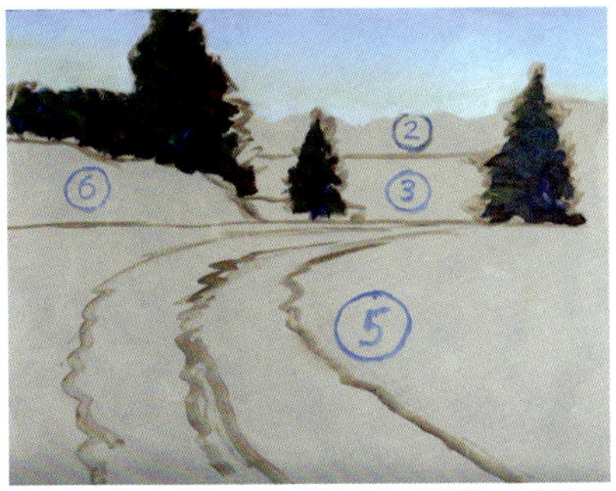

1. First block in the darks in the evergreens (4) in various dark colors, not completely blended together. I used colors like viridian, alizarin crimson, ultramarine, burnt umber and dark violet. Next we start with a greenish cold winter sky (1). I used cobalt blue, cadmium yellow light and white.

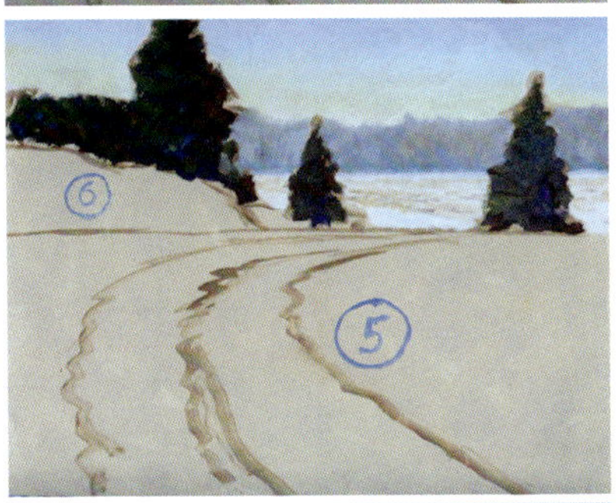

2. The distant trees are painted next with soft edges in violet, viridian, white and a little yellow ochre (2). You can use other subtle colors to create the effect of many trees. I also painted the fields (3) with white and yellow ochre to indicate the corn stubble sticking out of the snow.

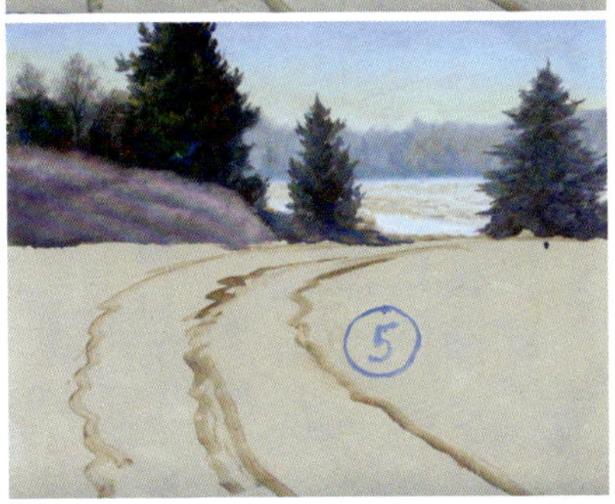

3. Now I finish the edges on my dark evergreens and added the scrubby trees on the left. Working forward I laid in the grayish pink Red Osier Dogwoods (6), using reds, violets, browns and white.

4. Using my palette knife I applied a lot of white, tinted just slightly with cadmium yellow and orange. I covered most of the foreground. Then using a mixture of burnt umber and cobalt blue, I added the shadows in the snow. I also created the curved tracks of the road by making the right sides dark, since the light came from the left. Switching to a brush, I blended some edges between the blue shadow and the white snow. The finishing touches include the yellow grasses sticking out of the snow, done with the edge of the palette knife. Most of the grasses were bent left by the wind. To emphasize the focal point, I found some burnt sienna and ochre grasses down by the end of the road. A few upward strokes with a big #12 brush accomplished that. Adding a few sky holes through the big evergreens and signing my name was all that was left to finish the piece.

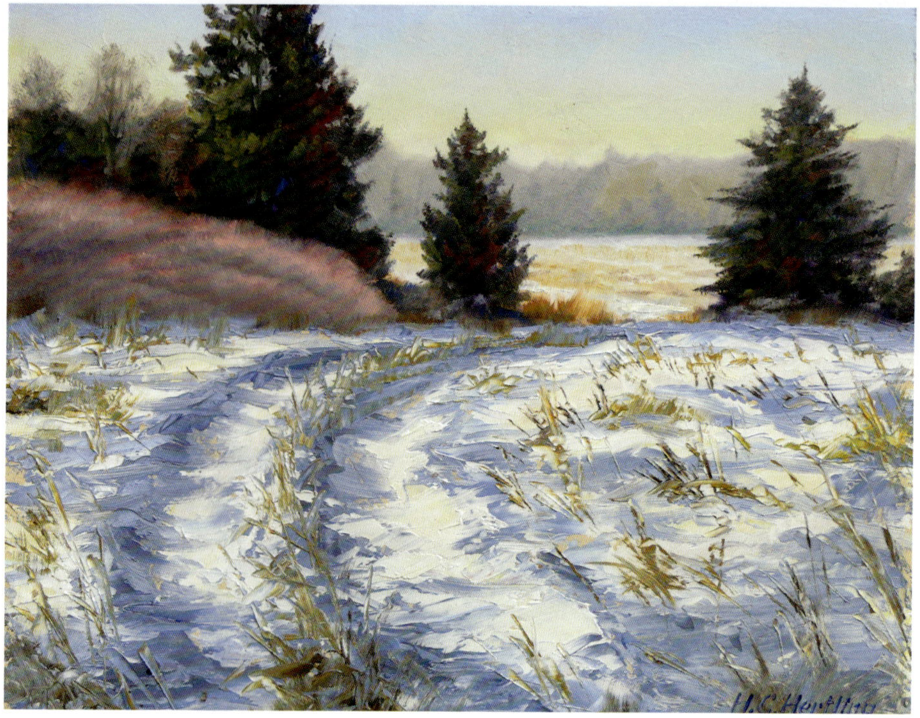

The Road Not Taken, 11 x 14 Oil

Finished Painting

TANGENTS

Bad tangents are something else to watch for! Remember that family photo where a church steeple was sticking out of grandpa's head? Or where an animal appears to have three legs because two of them were lined up right behind each other? Tangents, in this case bad ones, are created by lines, edges or shapes meeting each other to create an unpleasant and confusing image.

But rejoice, those things are fixable. You can just move objects around until they don't interfere with each other. The good thing is that they'll normally show up in your preliminary sketch before you start painting. If you don't see them right away ask somebody else. They might see the tangents because they have a "fresh eye" (another art term).

WRAP UP

I have shared a lot of my personal painting experiences with you. It is such a delightful way to spend precious time and like all arts, it enriches your life. It has to be shared. Schneepel, that little watercolor critter, kept us from getting too serious. Since painting reflects your emotional status, your feelings will show in your paintings, too. When you are happy and satisfied, a fine subject in bright colors may show up. When depressed or sad, it might show itself in a somber subject and subdued colors. That's okay, it has to be like that. You want to share with people some of yourself and if you don't let them in, it will not happen. Don't be afraid of failure. The further away the goal, the more satisfying when you reach it. I hope that's true for golf.

After cutting back from commercial art a few years ago, I found the time to try things that always intrigued me, sculpting in clay for bronzes, teaching painting workshops, carving in wood, building frames and learning to gild them. Now I am painting on TV and writing. There is no end.

I don't agree with that "no end" part. Look at my flat cousin on the road. Oh well, never mind. I'm going to try my paw at painting now. It should be an adventure!

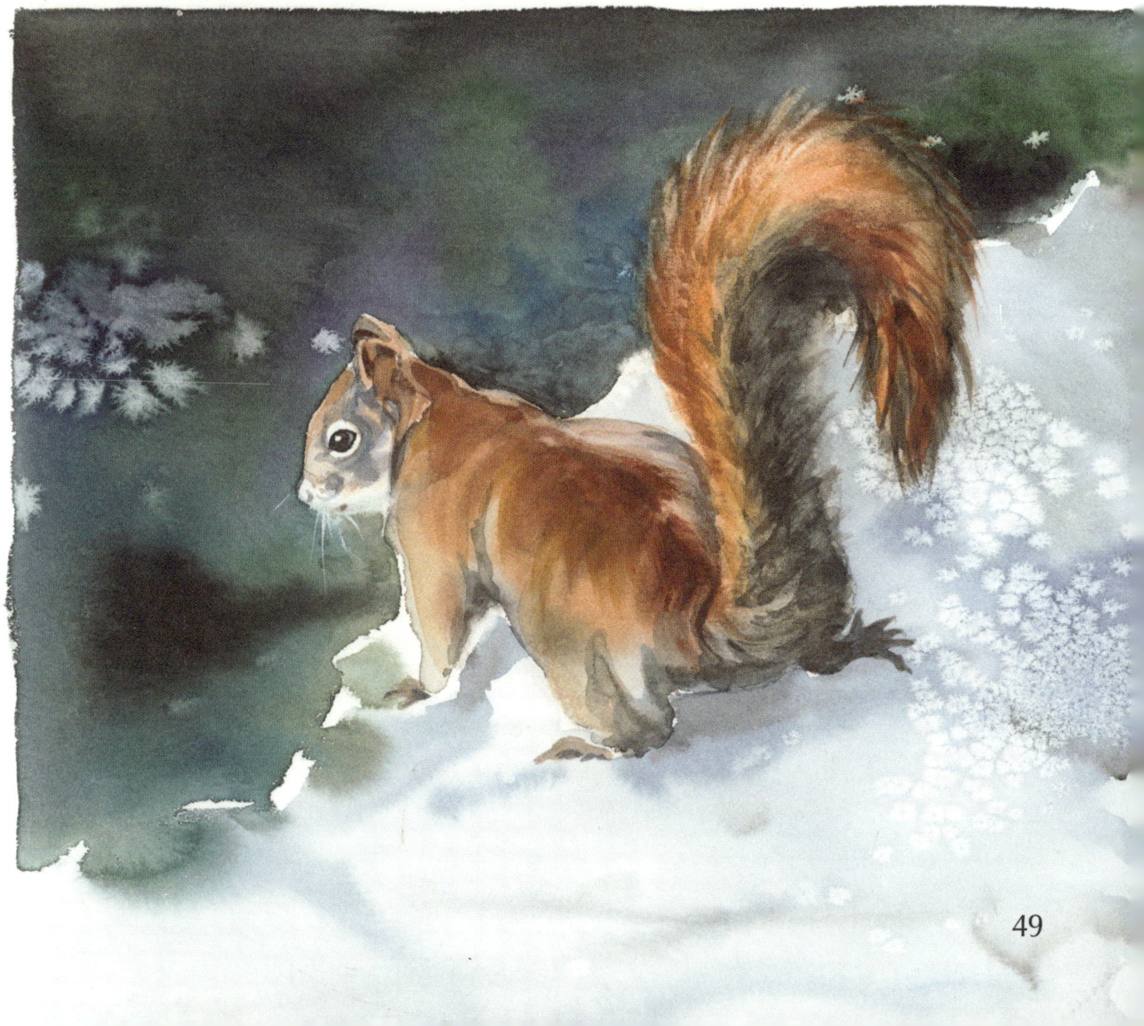

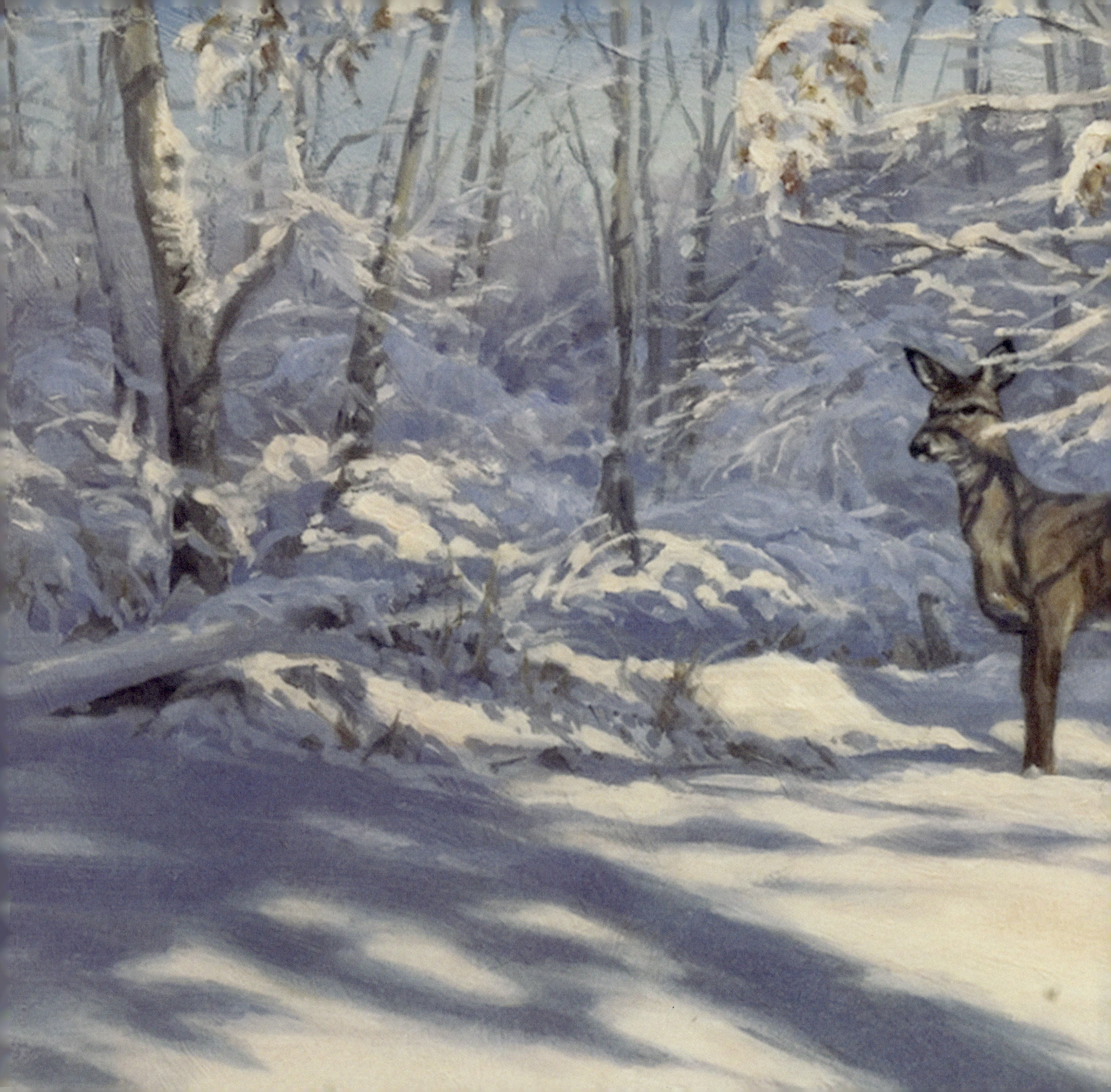